Shakespeare
Man of the Theater

Wendy Greenhill

Head of Education
Royal Shakespeare Company

Paul Wignall

Heinemann Library
Chicago, Illinois

Published by Heinemann Library,
an imprint of Reed Educational & Professional Publishing,
100 N. LaSalle, Suite 1010
Chicago, IL 60602
Customer Service 888-454-2279
Visit our website at www.heinemannlibrary.com

Greenhill, Wendy, 1949-
    Shakespeare : man of the theater / Wendy Greenhill, Paul Wignall.
        p. cm.
    Includes bibliographical references and index.
    Summary: Presents the life of William Shakespeare, describing his early years, his
development as a poet and playwright, and the historical context in which he lived and worked.
    ISBN 1-57572-282-8
        1. Shakespeare, William, 1564-1616—Juvenile literature. 2. Dramatists, English—Early
modern, 1500-1700—Biography—Juvenile literature. 3.
Theaters—England—London—History—17th century—Juvenile literature. 4.
Theaters—England—London—History—16th century—Juvenile literature. 5.
Theater—England—London—History—17th century—Juvenile literature. 6.
Theater—England—London—History—16th century—Juvenile literature. [1. Shakespeare,
William, 1564-1616. 2. Authors, English. 3. Theater—England—History—16th century.] I.
Wignall, Paul. II. Title.

PR2895.G76 2000
822.3'3—dc21
[B]   00-022245

Illustrations by Jeff Edwards
Printed by Wing King Tong in Hong Kong

04 03 02 01 00
10 9 8 7 6 5 4 3 2 1

Acknowledgments
The Publishers would like to thank the following for permission to
reproduce photographs:
Bibliothek der Reichsuniversitet, Utrecht, pp. 71, 108; Edinburgh University Library,
p. 5; Mary Evans Picture Library, p. 44; The Public Records Office, London, p. 174;
Shakespeare Birthplace Trust, Stratford, pp. 1, 21, 155; by permission of The Trustees
of Dulwich Picture Gallery, pp. 55, 112.

Cover photograph: Portrait of Shakespeare, from the title page of First Folio,
published in 1623, reproduced by permission of The Shakespeare Birthplace Trust,
Stratford-upon-Avon.

Some words are shown in bold, **like this**. You can find out what they mean by looking
in the glossary.

CONTENTS

I
Introduction: A Procession in London, 1604

At 11:00 A.M. on March 15, 1604, an enormous procession began to wind its way from the Tower of London. Everyone there counted themselves part of the royal court, including the entire government of England—bishops, knights, judges, barons, earls, and viscounts. At Barking Churchyard, they were greeted by songs from the children of Christ's Hospital School. They marched along Fenchurch Street, Gracechurch Street, and into Cheapside, where the great conduit which supplied the citizens with clean water was running with claret wine. They marched past St. Paul's Cathedral and along Fleet Street until at Temple Bar they left the City of London and entered Westminster. Up the strand they walked, past the fine houses of the most powerful noblemen of the kingdom, to Charing Cross. Then the procession continued on to Westminster Abbey until, turning left, they entered the Palace of Whitehall.

In the center of the procession rode King James I of England. He had been proclaimed king almost exactly 12 months earlier, following the death of Queen Elizabeth I. Traveling south from Scotland, where he was already king, James had not gone immediately to Westminster for fear of the **plague,** which was raging there. His coronation in Westminster Abbey on July 25, 1603 had little ceremony, also because of the plague. This day, March 15, 1604, was the first official opportunity for the large crowds lining the route in London to see their new king.

King James I in the Royal Procession, March 15, 1604, as shown in an illustration from Michael van Meer's *Album Amicorum.*

The procession from the Tower to Whitehall was a show of strength. The spectacle, and the official speeches and poems read along the way, displayed the magnificence of the king and the power of England. The foreign ambassadors among the cheering crowds were expected to be impressed by what they saw. Hopefully, they would report to their own kings that England was not a country with which to be trifled.

But behind the show of strength and unity, all was not well. The London through which James rode that March afternoon in 1604 was like a miniature of the condition of England. There was poverty in its narrow streets and lanes. There were merchants made rich by trade. There was the nobility, who were desperate to maintain status by this show of magnificence, which was being financed by a debt-ridden king.

When James became its king, England was undergoing painful social and economic changes. It is estimated that in the previous 50 years, the population increased from about three million to around four million. The growth in the number of mouths to feed was not matched by increased food production. This led to a rise in prices and a drop in wages. Families began to move around the country looking for work. The subsistence economy of the medieval countryside, where families and villages produced enough for their own needs, was replaced by a market economy, in which larger landowners supplied the food for a price and bought the farms of those struggling to survive. The rural England through which James traveled from Scotland in 1603 was a place of poverty, starvation, and discontent. From time to time, it erupted into open rebellion against the wealthier families.

These families, called the **gentry,** were the new force in the land. As they gained more economic power, they expected to exercise greater political power. In the later years of Queen Elizabeth I's reign, the House of Commons, which was made up of the land-owning gentry and influential merchants, demanded that its voice be heard. The traditional authority of the king or queen and the great noblemen dated back to the Middle Ages. It was being challenged by a more modern attitude. The gentry and the merchants, who supplied and organized the wealth of the nation, wanted to have their hands on the reins of power. They wanted to control the overspending of the royal court.

There were other pressures on James. The bishops of the Church of England, who walked ahead of him in the procession, were reminders of two other controversies. King Henry VIII's separation of the Church in England from the authority of the Pope in Rome in 1534 had plunged the country into religious discontent. For the next 30 years, there were open power struggles between **Catholics** and **Protestants.** Elizabeth had tried to bring the two sides together, but in reality she was ruling a people divided by their religion. It was believed, or imagined, that Catholics were plotting to overthrow the monarch in favor of a candidate who would restore Catholicism. Religious belief became a test of loyalty. To be a Catholic was to be suspected of treason.

If some of the citizens of London who greeted James with outward shows of loyalty were in fact secret Catholics, many others were openly **Puritan.** Puritanism had developed during the 1500s as a form of Christianity whose followers believed that people should have a direct relationship with God. This relationship, they felt, should be expressed in a simple, moral way of life that would purify society. **Puritans** were men and women trying to lead a good and honest life. They believed in hard work and disliked any outward show or extravagance in religion or in public or private life. Throughout James's reign, they were bitter opponents of his overspending and what they saw as the immorality of his court. The Puritans and their sympathizers in the gentry and merchant classes increasingly held the country's purse strings, much to James's irritation. After his death in 1625, their opposition to the new king, Charles I, gradually intensified. It erupted into civil war in which the Puritans were victorious. Charles was executed in 1649. He was replaced as head of state by Oliver Cromwell, who had been a leader of the king's parliamentary opponents.

The London through which James rode in March 1604, like the England he had traveled across a year earlier, was a place of contradiction. The old order—authority of the nobility and absolute rule of the king—was under threat from a new and increasingly powerful political and religious alliance of landowners and merchants.

Beneath the thin unity that the royal procession was intended to establish and reinforce, was a seething mass of discontent. It was fed by poverty, overcrowding, and starvation, as well as by religious disagreements and traitorous plotting. No wonder that concealed beneath the fine silks of his clothing, James wore, as he always did, a quilted jacket. It was padded to protect him from an assassin's knife.

THE KING'S MEN

Somewhere near the front of the procession, among the grooms and gentlemen of the royal household, there was a group of nine men. They wore crimson cloaks made of material specially provided for the occasion. They were the king's own company of actors called the King's Men. Their royal authority, received on May 19, 1603, read:

> Know ye that we... have licensed and authorised... these our servants Lawrence Fletcher, William Shakespeare, Richard Burbage, Augustine Phillips, John Heminges, Henry Condell, William Sly, Robert Armin, Richard Cowley, and the rest of their associates freely to use and exercise the art and faculty of playing comedies, tragedies, histories, interludes, morals, pastorals, stage-plays, and such others like... as well for the recreation of our loving subjects, as for our solace and pleasure when we shall think good to see them...

This document tells a great deal about the status and conditions of actors, or players as they were known, at the beginning of the 1600s.

1. The King's Men were licensed. Like all players they were controlled by the state and protected by powerful noblemen. The plays they performed were censored by a state official, the **Master of the Revels**, on behalf of the **Lord Chamberlain**.

2. Companies of players were part of the household of their **patrons**, but they were also independent. The nine men named in James's letter were **sharers** in the company. This meant that they were entitled to a part of the proceeds from the performances they gave. They might employ other players or train young players, but the risks and the profits were theirs. They were businessmen, as well as players or writers.

3. From our modern point of view, the theatrical life in the London of Elizabeth I and James I is overwhelmingly dominated by one name—William Shakespeare. It is important to remember, though, that this is not how it would have appeared to his contemporaries. He was one among many. He was one of nine **sharers** in the King's Men. He wrote plays for them—about two each year—but so did many other writers. He acted in those plays in the early years of their time together, and many of the sharers in the King's Men had been colleagues in one company or another for more than ten years before they became the king's company.

Shakespeare became wealthy because of his shares in the company, but so did all the others. However, today, Shakespeare seems to be a special case. His plays are still performed, moving audiences to tears or making them laugh, while the plays of many of his contemporaries gather dust on library shelves. Shakespeare cannot be properly understood if we don't also understand that in his day he was a professional actor, a businessman, and a courtier. His work reflects the world around him.

4. Players were expected to have a wide range of plays to perform. The demands of playgoers, from the king to the groundlings who paid a few pennies to stand and watch, were insatiable. New plays, in many styles, rolled off the production line faster than today's Hollywood movies. A playwright might produce three, four, or more plays a year. He might produce them alone or in collaboration with others. And companies competed with each other to come up with a hit. They were in the business of pleasing audiences.

5. Players had a number of audiences. There were the public playhouses in London—The Globe, The Fortune, The Rose, and others. There were the regular tours around the country, especially when the **plague** closed the London theaters. There were performances for players' **patrons** in the great country houses or in London. And there were the performances at court commanded by the king himself, either as part of the annual festivities at Christmas or for the entertainment of foreign ambassadors and princes. The King's Men in particular were not only in the business of pleasing their audience, they also had to please the king.

Of course, pleasing can be a challenge. The playhouses —as theaters were called—shared the same stresses and strains as the rest of society. The plays not only gave their audiences a comforting glimpse of national unity and authority, but they disclosed discontent within society. They showed fears bubbling beneath the surface. Playhouses were seen as dangerous places.

THE MIRROR UP TO NATURE

What was the place of the theater in the England of Elizabeth and James and of William Shakespeare? First of all, it was on the edges of society, both in fact and in people's imagination. The first playhouses were built in the **Liberties,** north of the city and on the south bank of the Thames River. They were called the Liberties because they were outside the bounds of the city's authority. This independence was reinforced, first by the support of noble patrons, including the king, and then by their popularity with playgoers. But plays and playhouses were marginal in a second sense. When Hamlet reminds the players that

> . . .the purpose of playing. . . was and is to hold as 'twere
> the mirror up to nature, to show virtue her own feature,
> scorn her own image, and the very age and body of the
> time his form and pressure. . .
>
> *Hamlet*, Act 3 Scene 2, lines 22–24

he is saying that in playhouses, playgoers see themselves reflected not as they would like to be, but as they are. The stage of the playhouse and the words the players speak capture the anxieties and fears, the joys and hopes of the world outside.

The society in which Shakespeare lived and worked was trapped between old ideas of authority and the demands of rapid social change. It was trapped between a king trying to embody unity through magnificent displays of power and seething discontent just below the surface. Put another way, Shakespeare's England could not avoid the gap between words and deeds. The wise person listened with a good dose of suspicion. In London and the Palace of Whitehall, which was the center of the king's court and government, survival meant knowing whom you trusted and knowing that you could trust almost no one.

Once again, the playhouses were the perfect place to reflect this war between trust and suspicion. Plays frequently reveal that gap between what we say we will do and what we actually do. That is to say, they depend upon **dramatic irony.** This irony is when an audience is aware of something that a character in the play is not aware of, be it a hidden dagger or a promise about to be broken.

Theater stands on the margins of society. When it is given enough freedom, it can show us as we are, not as we think we are. It does so by revealing the gap between what we say we will do and what we may actually do. But theater also shows us how we can be, when we are at our best, and what happens when the gap between words and deeds has been closed. Theater shows us what happens when we learn to trust. In Shakespeare's working life, he moved constantly between the language of suspicion and the language of trust. Judging by the plays he wrote at the time of the king's procession in March 1604, Shakespeare was perhaps at that time his most suspicious and cynical.

FOUR PLAYS

Four plays from these years have a vein of cynicism. They raise uncomfortable moral questions about love, sex, politics, and war. In *Measure for Measure* and *Macbeth*, Shakespeare explores problems of kingship. In *Troilus and Cressida* and in *Timon of Athens*, he shows the destructive descent from sexual love and wealth into suspicion and cynicism.

Lack of trust is a keynote throughout these plays. People eavesdrop and spy, trick and deceive, conceal and evade. Sex is traded for money, for favors, and for survival. Ideals dissolve in the tough world of lust, politics, and war. These plays all question the nature of love and the possibility of fidelity. They take a skeptical view of politics and morals. Everything and everyone has its price.

TROILUS AND CRESSIDA

The action of *Troilus and Cressida* takes place during the war between Ancient Greece and Troy. This is also the subject of one of the oldest and greatest works of

Western literature, *The Iliad*. Parts of this epic poem, written nearly 2,000 years earlier by Homer, had been translated by George Chapman in 1598. It immediately became a bestseller. It is the story of a war fought over Helen, the most beautiful woman in the world, and the wife of a Greek king. Helen has been abducted and taken to Troy by one of the Trojan king's sons. The Greeks follow and besiege the city to get her back.

Shakespeare's play takes place in the middle of the siege. It concerns a love affair between the Trojan, Troilus, and the Greek, Cressida. Their love is encouraged by Cressida's uncle, Pandarus, but broken by wider political considerations. Pandarus's cynicism twists the love of Troilus and Cressida into a nasty sexual grope. The vicious satire of the Greek soldier Thersites changes the bravery of the warriors into a tawdry fight among men for a woman who is not deserving. Even the final battle between the two great heroes, Achilles the Greek and Hector the Trojan, degenerates into mere brutality. Hector is surrounded by Achilles and Achilles' men, the Myrmidons.

> **Hector:** I am unarmed. Forgo this vantage, Greek.
> **Achilles:** Strike, fellows, strike. This is the man I seek
>
> *[The Myrmidons kill Hector]*
>
> So, Ilium, fall thou. Now, Troy, sink down.
> On Myrmidons, and cry you all amain,
> "Achilles hath the mighty Hector slain!"
>
> *Troilus and Cressida*, Act 5 Scene 9, lines 9–14

Thersites' language has images of disease, of turning Troy into a **plague**-ridden city, and of giving love the colors of death.

Thersites: Now the rotten diseases of the south, guts-
griping, ruptures, catarrhs, loads o' gravel
i' th' back, lethargies, cold palsies, and the
like, take and take again such preposterous
discoveries.

Troilus and Cressida, Act 5 Scene 1, lines 17–21

Troilus and Cressida is an astonishing play, remorselessly burying human values under lust, lying, death, and disease.

MEASURE FOR MEASURE

Shakespeare makes the city of Vienna, in which *Measure for Measure* is set, as full of infection as Troy. Perhaps disease was on his mind, as the London theaters had been closed from May 1603 to April 1604 because of plague. It is likely that the play was written some months after the theaters reopened. It was for certain played before James on December 26, 1604.

The play concerns Isabella, a young woman about to enter a nunnery. Her brother, Claudio, has been harshly condemned to death for immorality. The Duke of Vienna has gone away leaving the vice-ridden city in the control of his strictly moral deputy, Angelo. Angelo is determined to clean things up. Isabella pleads for Claudio's life, and Angelo, overcome with lust for her, agrees to spare Claudio if she will sleep with him. She appears to agree, but Angelo is tricked when another woman (Mariana, whom Angelo has abandoned) comes to him instead. The Duke returns, punishes Angelo for his hypocrisy, forces him to marry Mariana, and marries Isabella himself.

The play is deeply serious, as well as full of humor. It is set in **brothels** and prisons. It explores sex, death, and the abuse of power. Yet, the wise ruler sees the truth and judges well. The play also shows the theatrical nature of kingship at this time. The Duke creates a dramatic scene in which to make known his judgments, much as King James liked to rule by dramatic effects. But if the play seems to offer King James a mirror for his own view of justice, it has many painful undercurrents. Every character is ambiguous. No one is wholly good, nor utterly bad. Perhaps Shakespeare wants to show that justice is not a simple matter. Justice has to take account of the fact that we are all "desperately human" (*Measure for Measure,* act 4 scene 2, line 147).

TIMON OF ATHENS

Modern scholarship has shown that *Timon of Athens* is almost certainly a collaboration between Shakespeare and Thomas Middleton, a playwright nearly 20 years younger. Middleton may well have had a hand in *Measure for Measure* and *Macbeth* as well, so it may be assumed that he worked closely with the King's Men after 1602. *Timon of Athens* may even be a revision of an original play by Middleton. It was probably written in 1604.

The play, as it is known now, is not unlike earlier, medieval plays that showed the journey of a good man through the temptations of life. But *Timon of Athens* is a grim story. It shows a rich and generous man's fall into poverty. As he falls, his friends abandon him. In the second part, he becomes rich again, but he is now bitter and leaves Athens in disgust.

Nothing I'll bear from thee
But nakedness, thou detestable town. . .
The gods confound—hear me you good gods all—
Th' Athenians, both within and out that wall;
And grant, as Timon grows, his hate may grow
To the whole race of mankind, high and low.
Amen.

Timon of Athens, Act 4 Scene 1, lines 32–40

Timon's bitterness drives him away from civilization, away from other people, and out into the desert. He prepares for death by digging his own grave and writing his epitaph. The pursuit of wealth, which was the basis of his former generosity and the cause of his fall, is now the focus of his contempt.

What a god's gold,
That he is worshipped in a baser temple
Than where swine feed!
To thee be worship, and thy saints for aye
Be crowned with plagues, that thee alone obey.

Timon of Athens, Act 5 Scene 1, lines 46–52

For Christianity the desert is traditionally the place where God is found. The wilderness is the place of truth. But at the end of his journey, Timon has no room for joy or comfort. His epitaph is a curse.

Seek not my name. A plague consume
    You wicked caitiffs left!
Here lie I, Timon, who alive
    All living men did hate.

Timon of Athens, Act 5 Scene 5, lines 73–76

MACBETH

The previous three plays are from Shakespeare's middle years. They are comparatively little known. Two are unfortunately rarely performed. The fourth play, *Macbeth*, is one of Shakespeare's most famous.

Macbeth was probably written in 1606. It explores the problems that terrified King James. The king lived in fear of assassination and of witchcraft. In *Macbeth*, a Scottish nobleman is encouraged by three weird witch sisters to kill King Duncan and take the throne. *Weird* is an old English word for fate or destiny. The women are "weird" because they foretell the future. Macbeth and his wife come to embody evil. The portrayal of their collapse under the weight of guilty consciences and their destruction by the forces of good would have pleased James. But, as always with Shakespeare, what seems to be simply a story of good overcoming evil is really much more complex.

Macbeth explores what it means to make choices. Should Macbeth and his wife be loyal to their king, or should they take the opportunity to seize power? The human capacity to choose is undercut by fate. The weird sisters' promise—that Macbeth will be king hereafter—seems to take away his duty to act morally. But this is a delusion. As the play unfolds the audience and with the Macbeths, become painfully aware that destiny and choice are two edges of the same sword.

As the play proceeds down its dark and murderous path, we are constantly asked to consider how much the Macbeths are responsible for what they do. Lady Macbeth seems to be the stronger of the two, but she is finally broken by the guilt she cannot easily acknowledge. Macbeth's conscience never lets him forget the difference between what he should have done and what he did do. He should not have killed Duncan. He should have chosen differently.

As the Macbeths embark on their career of murder, a gap begins to open between the way they must behave in public and their private world of guilt and fear. They are mistaken if they think they can leave their consciences behind. But as public figures, exercising power, and as actors on the political stage, they must do so. *Macbeth* gives little hope that kings can sleep easy in their beds. Their role is intolerable. They cannot wash the blood from their hands. In the end Lady Macbeth dies, unable to deal with the pressure of guilt. As he hears of her death, Macbeth accepts the futility of what he has done.

> Life's but a walking shadow, a poor player
> That struts and frets his hour upon the stage,
> And then is heard no more. It is a tale
> Told by an idiot, full of sound and fury,
> Signifying nothing.
>
> *Macbeth*, Act 5 Scene 5, lines 23–27

2
STRATFORD-UPON-AVON

The precise date of William Shakespeare's birth is not known. However, his name appears in the register of baptisms of Holy Trinity Church in Stratford-upon-Avon on April 26, 1564. Children were usually baptized within two or three days of their birth, and tradition has put Shakespeare's birthday as April 23.

What type of place was Stratford, England, in 1564? Like most English market towns, Stratford owed its growth first to the fact that 368 years earlier, in 1196, it had been granted the status of a **borough**. This gave the **burgesses,** who were the people living there, certain rights and privileges. As freemen, burgesses controlled their towns independently of the great landowners. They were not tied to the land, but bought local farmers' products and sold them near and far. Burgesses might also manufacture goods from some of the locally produced raw materials, again selling them both locally and across England.

Such towns were usually situated at strategic communication points. Stratford's bridge over the Avon River was built in about 1490 with money provided by Sir Hugh Clopton. He also built New Place, Shakespeare's Stratford home from 1597 to 1616. The bridge, which is still one of the main routes through Stratford, gave a boost to the town's trading connections between central England and London.

By the time the Clopton Bridge was built, Stratford's life was largely controlled by the **Guild** of the Holy Cross. This was an association of town tradesmen, merchants, and local landowning **gentry**. The Guild

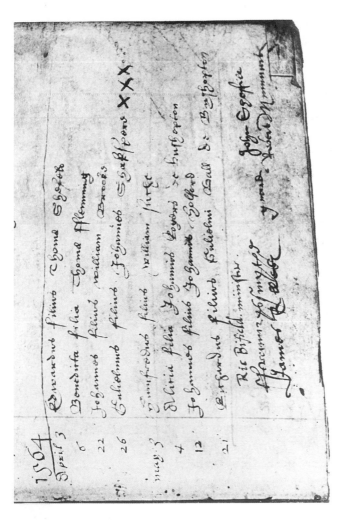

A page of the Stratford baptism register for 1564. Near the bottom is Gulielmus filius Johannes Shakspear, which means "William, son of John Shakespeare." The register is now in The Shakespeare Birthplace Trust, Stratford-upon-Avon.

managed the town's prosperity to the advantage of those who created the prosperity, but the **Guild** also provided for the public good. By 1547, the Guild's responsibility included repairs to the bridge and building and maintaining almshouses, which are special accommodations for the poor and elderly. They also funded the town's **grammar school**.

In 1547, 17 years before William Shakespeare was born, great social changes came to Stratford. These were triggered partly by the religious upheaval of the **Reformation** and partly by the new economic conditions in England. The Guild of the Holy Cross, along with many other religious foundations, was abolished. Its property was taken by the king. The town was left in a state of chaos until 1553 when the new king, Edward VI, granted a charter for a new arrangement in Stratford.

The Guild's duties were taken over by a **bailiff** and fourteen **aldermen.** The bailiff and aldermen were prominent local men. They became responsible for the bridge, the almshouses, the school, and for paying the **vicar.** The property taken from the Guild was returned to help the new Corporation carry out its duties. It was also allowed to appoint 14 burgesses, who were other townsmen. They were given particular duties. Two burgesses, for example, were required to keep account of the town's finances and property. In 1564 these responsible posts were held by John Taylor and John Shakespeare.

JOHN SHAKESPEARE AND MARY ARDEN

To understand William Shakespeare as a playwright, landowner, trader, father, husband, and **sharer** in an important theater company, then we have to understand something of his background. In his background were the expectations and ambitions of his family and society.

John and Mary Shakespeare, William's parents, were typical of those who created, prospered under, and sometimes became the victims of the great changes of the 1500s. Their story does not explain their son's exceptional gifts as a poet and playwright, but it may give an idea of how he used those gifts to make his way in the world.

William's grandfather, Richard Shakespeare, was a tenant farmer at Snitterfield, a village four miles north of Stratford. His landlord was Richard Arden of Wilmcote, a village west of Stratford, about three miles away. By the 1540s, Richard Shakespeare was fairly prosperous. By the time of his death in 1560, he had become an influential and wealthy man. His story shows how it was possible for tenant farmers to climb the social and economic ladder during the boom years in the middle of the 1500s.

Richard Shakespeare's son, John, moved to Stratford as a young man. He became a glover, someone who makes gloves, and a whittawer, a worker in expensive white leather.

Leather-making and leather-working were two of the most important trades in the Midlands of England in the 1500s. Some of Stratford's wealthiest citizens were associated with it. John was probably **apprenticed** to Thomas Dickson, who had family connections in Snitterfield. Whatever the precise and personal reasons for his move, it was typical of the time that the son of a successful tenant farmer would become an apprentice in a trade. In the trades, he could learn a skill and make the family's life better.

Leather-making is a good example of the new prosperity. Glovers bought animal skins, prepared them by the process of tanning, then turned them into a range of goods. They made gloves, belts, and bags. Like most trades, it required money to buy the skins and to make the finished product. As in most trades, the tradesman worked at or near his home. When John Shakespeare set up his shop in Henley Street in Stratford before 1552, it was accepted that he would live above the shop. Some of the smellier parts of the tanning process, which used raw materials, such as urine and alum, were probably done elsewhere in Stratford.

By 1557, John Shakespeare was ready to marry. Once more he called on family connections. Mary Arden was seventeen. She was a daughter of the late Richard Arden of Wilmcote, who had been Richard Shakespeare's landlord. We do not know where the Ardens lived in Wilmcote. The place now visited by tourists as Mary Arden's House never had any connection with the family. However, that house is typical of the type of place where the Ardens would have lived.

Mary Arden must have been a capable young woman. When her father died in December 1556, she took charge of the property arrangements. She also inherited some of her father's land. John Shakespeare may have fallen in love with her, but he also made a practical choice. She was wealthy, and her income, which legally passed to John, would have enabled him to keep his business growing. Mary could also run a household and was experienced in managing property and money. She became not only John's wife, but also his business partner.

This was typical of the time. The relationship between men and women in marriage was changing in the 1500s. Traditionally, legally, and very often in reality, a man expected obedience from his wife and children. But reformed Christianity in the 1500s was beginning to stress the importance of companionship in marriage. Husband and wife were still a long way from being equals, but women had important roles to play. They shared in the responsibilities and duties of households. Of course there were those who thought the changes were upsetting a fundamental, God-given order. The woman's place was to be obedient to her husband. But in fact it was impossible to run any complex household unless husbands and wives shared day-to-day decision-making.

The gap between the public assertion of patriarchy, or rule by men, and the reality of marriages as practical partnerships led to a good deal of anxiety. This was expressed both in jokes and cautionary stories about dominant women. The relationship between men and women in love and the preparation for marriage was to become one of the most important themes in many of Shakespeare's plays.

THE RISE OF JOHN SHAKESPEARE

As a rising young glover, John Shakespeare needed to play a part in Stratford's public life. In 1556, he was an official beer taster. Two years later he was a constable keeping the peace. The next year he was an affeeror. This meant he assessed the fines that citizens had to pay. In 1561, he became one of the 14 **burgesses** or town councilors. In 1564, the year of William's birth, he rose to the position of **Chamberlain** and was in charge of the town's finances.

John was obviously liked and trusted. In 1565, he was elected one of the 14 **aldermen,** the senior officials who ran Stratford. Three years later, on October 1, 1568, he took the post of **bailiff** for the year. This was the key post in the town. In the 16 years since his first mention in the Stratford records, when he was fined in 1552 for keeping a dunghill in Henley Street, John had risen to a position of trust in his adopted home town.

THE SHAKESPEARE FAMILY

William was the third child and eldest son of the eight sons and daughters of John and Mary Shakespeare. Their first child, Joan, was born in 1558 and died as an infant. In 1562, another daughter, Margaret, was born, but she died a year later. William came next in April 1564. Within months, the **plague** was raging, killing old and young alike. Nearly 20 percent of the population of Stratford died of the plague in the second half of 1564. John and Mary's anxiety, that their first son would follow his sisters to an early grave, can be easily imagined.

The next child, Gilbert, was born in October 1566. He

never married. William's story might well have been the same as Gilbert's, except William had talent as a player and writer. Gilbert was a successful businessman with interests in London and Stratford. He died in February 1612.

Joan Shakespeare, named for her deceased sister, was born in April 1569. She married, became Joan Hart, remained in Stratford, had three sons, and died in 1646 at the age of 76.

John and Mary's next child, Anne, was born in September 1571. She died at the age of seven in April 1579. We know almost nothing about their son Richard, except that he was born in March 1574 and died in Stratford in February 1613.

The eighth and last child, Edmund, was baptized on May 3, 1580. He followed William to London where he became a player. He died in December 1607 at the age of 27. He was buried in the church of St. Mary Overy, near The Globe Theatre, on the south bank of the Thames River. Edmund made no name for himself as an actor, but the funeral was expensive. Presumably it was paid for by his older brother, William.

The children of John and Mary Shakespeare are typical of a prosperous small town family of their time. Some died young, but one lived to be 76. Those who grew to be adults kept more or less strong links with their home town. But the sons also had links with London, the center of English life and trade. They differ little from the families of many other successful merchants and tradesmen living in the market towns of England in the 1500s. Only the remarkable career of one son lifts this family out of obscurity.

SHAKESPEARE AT SCHOOL

John and Mary Shakespeare were quite possibly unable to read or write. Their business as glovers, and John's involvement with town affairs, were conducted by word of mouth. This was not unusual. If they needed legal documents, then they would call a lawyer or a clerk. But the newly prosperous merchant and tradesmen families valued education for their sons. All over England, grammar schools were established. Many of them replaced church or cathedral schools.

In Stratford in 1553, responsibility for the school passed from the old **guild** to the new town corporation. One of the advantages of being a **burgess** was that your children could be educated at the school free of charge. There is no proof, but it is almost certain, that John Shakespeare would have made use of this privilege. Sometime in 1570, when he was six, William Shakespeare probably began a course of education lasting for eight or nine years.

The **bailiff** and **aldermen** of Stratford paid their schoolmaster well and attracted good teachers. If Shakespeare was at the school in 1570 when he was six, then the master was Walter Roche, although the youngest pupils were usually taught by an assistant. When Roche left in 1571, he was replaced by Simon Hunt, who remained for four years. Between 1575 and 1579, the master was Thomas Jenkins. Jenkins was an Oxford University graduate who had spent the past nine years as a teacher in Warwick. When Jenkins left, he named as his successor John Cottom, another Oxford man. Cottom remained until 1581, when he returned to his home in Lancashire.

It is possible that Simon Hunt had **Catholic** leanings. A man of that name arrived at the Catholic university at Douai in modern Belgium in 1575 and became a **Jesuit** in Rome in 1578. It is certain that John Cottom was a Catholic. His brother Thomas, a Jesuit, was thought to be a spy. Thomas was arrested in England in 1580 as he carried a letter addressed to a man in Shottery, a village just outside Stratford. Thomas was tried in November 1581 and executed in May 1582. Perhaps John Cottom returned to Lancashire to avoid problems from his brother's trial and death. These connections give some idea as to what William Shakespeare did after he left school.

When John Shakespeare moved from his father's home in Snitterfield to become a glover in Stratford, his opinions, knowledge, and attitudes would be similar to those he left behind. When William Shakespeare walked the few hundred yards through Stratford from his home in Henley Street to the grammar school in the Guild Hall he was entering another world.

To have a grammar school education was not only to learn the skills of reading and writing. It also opened up a world of learning and attitudes to life that separated schoolboys forever from their parents. School days were long. Mornings were from 6:00 or 7:00 in the morning until 11:00 A.M. The afternoons were from 1:00 to 5:00 P.M. and had two main elements.

First the boys learned Latin grammar. Then they learned a collection of useful words, phrases, and simple ideas. Finally they put these to use by writing increasingly complicated Latin sentences. From the age of nine they would also be reading and translating

political speeches by the ancient Roman author
Cicero, poems of Virgil and Ovid, plays of Terence
and Plautus, and dialogues and letters composed in
Latin and collected by the modern author Erasmus.
This material was intended to help the boys think
clearly and deeply about the world around them. It
also acted as a model for their own speech and writing.
Latin was the language of diplomacy, law, and
learning. No one could be thought of as educated if
they did not know Latin. Shakespeare's plays and
poems are filled with references to the Latin books he
would have read and learned by heart at school.

But the **grammar schools** were educating boys for a
new world in which their own language, English, was
also being much more highly valued. It seems quite
possible that both Richard Jenkins and John Cottom
were influenced as teachers by one of the most radical
and famous schoolmasters of the 16th century,
Richard Mulcaster. Mulcaster taught at the Merchant
Taylor's School in London. It was his aim to do for the
English language what traditional education did for
Latin. He wanted to make young men confident in
using their own language. He wrote, "I love Rome, but
London better. I favor Italy, but England more. I
honor the Latin, but I worship the English."

Mulcaster's method had a second significant element.
He believed that education was about the confident
use of the spoken word as well as the written language.
So he encouraged drama in his schools. His boys were
to learn, through acting, the tricks of good, persuasive
speech. This gave a particular energy to Mulcaster's
system of education. Boys stood up, acting plays,

scenes, or dialogues in fresh modern English as often as they sat at desks studying their Latin texts.

Education in the grammar schools was first and foremost about using language confidently and precisely. But education was very practical, too. The skilled use of language would enable boys to be persuasive in their arguments, to win in disputes, to get their point of view across to others. Education was about **rhetoric**—the art of persuasion.

This was nothing new. Rhetoric had always been part of the school curriculum. But its study had gained new energy in the late 1500s and 1600s. For instance, Rudolph Agricola wrote in 1479, "The aim of language is to make someone share your own view . . . the speaker should be understood, the listener should be persuaded to listen eagerly. . . Grammar deals with the principles of correct and clear speech, rhetoric teaches us to be elegant and interesting in our speech—making traps for capturing ears." Studying Latin authors was intended to provide these skills.

English education in the 1500s showed how persuasive techniques could be found in everyday language. These techniques were in the conversations of the marketplace and the inn, and in the letters that were an increasingly important means of communication. Shakespeare learned these lessons well. Throughout his plays and poems, the tricks and traps of rhetoric are used to persuade for good and for bad.

CATHOLICS AND PROTESTANTS

Throughout the 1500s, religion was one of the great dividing lines of English society. Once King Henry VIII provoked the final break with the Pope in 1534, English people had to choose between the old, **Catholic** form of Christianity and the newer, **Protestant** ways of belief and worship. The side they chose was also an indication of their political allegiance. Religious changes affected the whole of life.

The changes were not simply the product of religious arguments. The growing power of merchants against the church and the rise of independent nation-states, such as England, against the authority of the Pope were preparing a fertile ground for the new order. But the crucial test of which side one was on was a religious one.

These religious arguments spilled into the life of Stratford in a number of very typical ways. First, the system of government, which had been closely linked with the church, was changed. The **Guild** of the Holy Cross was replaced by the corporation of **bailiff** and **aldermen.** Second, the outward show of religious and social life was altered. Church services began to be in English, not Latin. Clergymen began to marry. The richly decorated churches became bare and simple. In January 1564, John Shakespeare, **chamberlain** of the town, paid workmen two shillings "for defacing images in the Chapel." The wall paintings in the Guild Chapel, once the home of the Guild of the Holy Cross and now where town officials worshipped, were hidden behind a coat of whitewash, which was not removed until 1804.

Stratford was late in taking this action. The government in London had ordered such things to be done four years earlier. The Guild Chapel paintings were covered over, but not destroyed as the government expected. Perhaps many Stratford citizens wanted to see the return of Catholicism as the religion of England.

John Shakespeare himself may have been one of these **recusants,** as they were called. Recusant comes from the Latin word *recuso,* meaning "I refuse." He may have played less of a part in town life after 1577 because he was sympathetic to Catholicism. Certainly by the 1590s, he was staying away from church. He was fined for this offense. Many Stratford families and some of the extended Shakespeare family were Catholic, including the Ardens. When William Shakespeare's Catholic cousin, John Somerville, was arrested in 1583, he was on his way to assassinate the queen.

None of this proves that John Shakespeare was a Catholic. He might have stayed away from church because he was in debt and was afraid of arrest. He may have ceased to be part of town life because of the decline in his business. But it appears that he had Catholic sympathies. This supports the theories about what happened to William Shakespeare in the years from leaving school in about 1580 to his arrival in London sometime before 1592. These are the so-called lost years.

THE LOST YEARS

William Shakespeare married Anne Hathaway of Shottery, near Stratford, in November 1582. She was eight years older than he. They married quickly, possibly because she was pregnant with their first child. This was Susanna, who was baptized in May 1583. Two years later William and Anne had twins,

Judith and Hamnet. They were baptized in January 1585. That is all that is known of those years.

Some of Shakespeare's biographers think there is a large gap in the story of his life. This gap is sometimes filled with wild speculation. Maybe he was a soldier and went abroad. Maybe he trained as a lawyer. Perhaps he trained as a schoolmaster or acted as a private tutor for a wealthy family. There are stories that he hunted deer at Charlecote, a few miles east of Stratford. There are drinking stories and traveling stories. They are all good stories, but there is no evidence to back them up.

Over the years, however, one group of ideas began to cluster into a story that some scholars think may account for these lost years. The stories link William's obvious intelligence, the possibility of learning to be an actor, and his father's likely **Catholicism.** Many people think these stories are more true than most.

Briefly the story is this: John Cottom, the Catholic schoolmaster, went back to Lancashire in 1581. What if Cottom thought highly of the bright boy from a Catholic family whom he had taught in Stratford? What if he recommended him to nearby Catholic families, the Hoghtons and the Heskeths? William might arrive in Lancashire as a schoolmaster with a desire to act. He may have seen the companies of players who visited Stratford during his childhood. Soon he is involved with the Hoghton family's own troupe of players. In August 1581, Alexander Hoghton's will refers to a servant called William Shakeshafte. This is not an impossible version of Shakespeare's name. Names were often spelled in different ways at this time. Could this be the Stratford boy?

The story asks us to think that Shakespeare was back in Stratford between 1582 and 1585. During those years, he married and had three children. Then with a wife and three children to support, and ambitions to satisfy, he seeks his fortune again as a player and playwright. He joins a company of players, Lord Strange's Men, that has strong connections with the same Lancashire Catholic families for whom he had been working. We know that many players in this acting company were also Shakespeare's close and lifelong colleagues in the Lord **Chamberlain's** Men and the King's Men.

All of this is speculation. But it does bring together some of the known facts of Shakespeare's life, and it makes sense of others. However, it also means that by the age of seventeen, Shakespeare was so established as a player that he could be referred to in Alexander Hoghton's will. Second, that after having got himself into this position, he gave it up to move back to Stratford, get married, and have three children. Third, he then rejoined a company of actors and worked with them in London, where he also began to write.

The story may seem possible, but it is not the only possibility. Shakespeare may have remained in Stratford, working with his father or assisting at his old school, and then married Anne Hathaway and had his children. There would have been plenty of opportunities to see companies of players in Stratford. There were frequent performances in the **Guild** Hall. In June 1587, one of the best companies, the Queen's

Men, had a problem. One of their actors, William Knell, was killed in a duel at Thame in Oxfordshire. It is not known whether the company was on its way to Stratford or had just left. It is possible that Shakespeare, either as a young hopeful or as an experienced actor, joined them.

By the late 1580s or early 1590s, Shakespeare had arrived on the London scene as a player and playwright. However he got there, he must somehow have learned his trade and convinced others of his skill. One element that helps to make up the so-called lost years is an **apprenticeship** with a company of players. This may have been through Lord Strange's Men or through the Queen's Men or a combination of both. What is known is that the lost years come to an end in 1592 when a dying playwright called Robert Greene attacked a new writer. The new writer was becoming more popular than Greene. Greene sarcastically told other established playwrights to beware.

> an upstart Crow, beautified with our feathers that . . . supposes he is as well able to bombast out a blank verse as the rest of you and. . . is in his own conceit the onely Shake-scene in a country . . . O that I might entreat your rare wits to be imploied in more profitable courses . . . I knowe the best husband of you will never prove a Usurer and the kindest of them all will never prove a kind nurse . . .

Greene's attack tells four important things about this writer. He is popular. He is a mere player as his writing has been learned on the job, not at the universities. He is a money-lender ("I know the best husband of you will never prove a Usurer [moneylender]"). He is William Shakespeare, "the only Shake-scene in a country."

By 1592, William Shakespeare had worked out his apprenticeship as a player and begun to write plays. His plays were popular enough to replace those of Robert Greene. He may have been linked with the Queen's Men or Lord Strange's Men, or both. Greene's plays were being replaced in the repertoires of both those companies by Shakespeare's plays during the early 1590s. Most interesting of all, he may have arrived in London to continue his father's business. We know that John Shakespeare was a moneylender as well as a glover, and that he traded in a range of goods. Every ambitious merchant needed a London connection. It appears that William Shakespeare pursued his own career and kept business connections with Stratford.

3
THE BEGINNINGS OF DRAMA

The impulse to tell stories is as old as humanity. Performing stories and watching others act them out is one of the most basic social activities.

For the ancient Greeks, drama was an outpouring of the dangerous power of the god Dionysus. This might take the form of rough, or even improvised, performances at planting time, harvest, weddings, or funerals. It might be a highly ritualized, skillfully acted, and carefully prepared event attended by all the citizens of a town. Either way, rough or skilled, the aim was ecstasy. Actors and onlookers alike were taken out of themselves. They were lifted into terror or delight by the power of the god. In the mirror of the stage, they saw themselves as they might wish or fear to be.

Plays were performed to mark the change of seasons or important moments in human life. They might also mark the historical moments of a village, a city, or a nation. Drama told stories to help communities understand who they were and from where they had come. The performances helped people take responsibility for their lives and deal with the unexpected.

Finally, drama was an outpouring of energy. It was never dull. Dramatic performances were like carnivals. They were dangerous, emotionally exhausting events. They were tidal waves that swept up individuals and whole communities.

Folk drama

The ancient Greek experience reminds us that drama began with the worship of gods. Long after the reasons for telling a story or doing a dance have been forgotten, the event itself remains in village festivals. England in the Middle Ages was full of such festivals. Many of them have lasted to the present day.

The Abbot's Bromley Horn in Staffordshire, for example, is a dance for men. The men wear ancient sets of deer antlers as they dance through their village. The Furry Dance in Helston and the Padstow Hobby dance, both in Cornwall, still draw crowds although their true purpose is almost forgotten. Towns and villages still have fairs or carnivals that date back to the worship of pre-Christian gods. Many of the dances include mock fights that originally acted out the battle between winter and summer or the battles between rival tribes. Other dances have links with fertility. Making crops grow or bringing the sexes together to start a new generation ensures that village life will go on. Some of these events took the form of plays, performed by **mummers** or **guisers**. The plays were often about Robin Hood or St. George. We know that in the 1500s, the people of Stratford watched a play every year about St. George and the Dragon.

These plays had combat, death, and rebirth, and they ended with a sword dance. They are part of the raw material that goes into the hugely energetic plays of Shakespeare and his contemporaries. Shakespeare's plays often end with a bawdy, sexually suggestive dance. Sometimes there are clear links to the cycles of nature. The comedy, *Love's Labour's Lost*, ends with two songs. One is about winter, and the other is about summer. *A Midsummer Night's Dream* ends with a **bergamasque** danced by the countrymen who have just performed at the wedding banquet. Even when not written in, and however alien to the mood of the play, it seems that audiences expected a dance. A performance of *Julius Caesar* in 1599 ended with just such a **jig** as an opportunity for the clowns to do their stuff.

DRAMA AND THE CHURCH

There has always been a close connection between drama and religion. Many folk traditions began as celebrations of pre-Christian gods. The growth of Christianity transferred some of these into the church. Christmas celebrations began as festivals at the turn of the year, when the sun began to climb back toward summer. Easter eggs are ancient symbols of fertility. Christian Church services are themselves dramas that tell the story of the death and resurrection of Jesus Christ. As the celebrations developed in magnificence and complexity, some other short plays grew out of them and began to stand alone. One of the first was enacted early on the morning of Easter Day. It showed the women finding the empty tomb of Jesus.

In 1311, the Church established a new festival. It was to become crucial to the development of drama, not only in England but also across Europe. Some years earlier, theologians had finally formulated a new understanding of the body and blood of Christ, which worshippers receive at the Holy Communion or Mass. They wanted to stress the miraculous way in which what was human became divine and how the bread and wine placed on the altar became Christ's body and blood. The Feast of **Corpus Christi**—from the Latin words meaning "the Body of Christ"—was established to present this doctrine to Christians. The new understanding required a new "drama" that would emphasize Christ's humanity. At the same time it would be a celebration of the human story.

By the middle of the 1300s, in many countries and English towns, cycles of plays had been developed. They told the story of God's dealings with the human race from the beginning to the end of history. The plays were deliberately a celebration, too, of humanity. Through them the Bible story characters became recognizable human beings. Costume, speech, settings, and characters were local. The aim of the plays was to show to the actors and the audience that characters in the Bible stories were no different from themselves and their neighbors. Shepherds in the fields outside Bethlehem complained about the taxman in Yorkshire accents. Carpenters used real hammers to nail Jesus to the cross.

These cycles of plays provided religious teaching. They also had three other characteristics. First, the plays were written in English and were produced and performed by local people. Each play was the responsibility of a particular group, such as the **guilds** or **mysteries** of craftsmen or merchants. This is why these dramas are often called mystery plays. Preparing and performing the dramas was an event in which the whole community joined. Second, in the plays, the everyday became a subject of drama that showed God's involvement here and now with human life. With wit and pathos, the plays showed the ordinary lives of the men and women in the towns where they were performed. Third, the **mystery** plays encouraged the development of the whole range of drama skills. People learned how to write dialogue, construct plots, and create sets, costumes, and props. Players began to understand how to portray characters and how to play to an audience.

In England, the **Corpus Christi** plays continued until 1548. That was when theological changes in the English church, after its break with Rome, led to the abolition of the plays. They were revived again when **Catholicism** was restored under Queen Mary, who was queen from 1553 to 1558. With the death of Queen Mary and the return of the **Protestant** religion, the plays were abolished again. The last performance until modern times of any of the English cycles was in Coventry in 1580. Coventry is just a few miles from Stratford. Was the 16-year-old William Shakespeare there to watch? It is possible, especially if his family were secretly Catholics. Even though the mystery cycles were abolished, their energy, their themes about ordinary people, and their theatrical skills lived on. Shakespeare was part of this.

POWER AND DISPLAY

One of the most effective ways in which the church communicated its message and its power over the lives of men and women was by the magnificence of its ceremonies. Priests, bishops, and popes wore expensive liturgical vestments. This clothing was encrusted with jewels and was beautifully embroidered. The churches where these ceremonies were held were usually among the largest buildings in a town. They had beautiful carvings and majestic stained-glass windows. Worshippers were supposed to be overawed by the power of God as represented by his Church on Earth.

Kings and princes, and later in the Middle Ages the merchants and town or city councils, tried in their own way to impress the people. They took their cue from the Church. The relationships between king and subject or between cities had to be shown and acted out. Processions and dramatic **pageants** showed a city's wealth and power just as its great buildings did.

The need to establish power relationships was never far away. During the 1500s, what has been called "the liturgy of state" gradually overtook the liturgical services of the Church in splendor and importance. When King James I processed through London in March 1604, the whole event was a carefully constructed piece of flattery. Temporary archways were built along the route. They were carved with symbols of the new king's wisdom and power. The procession was periodically halted while companies of actors performed in the king's honor.

The procession through London was a local form of another important royal event, the **progress**. In the progress, monarchs traveled through the country in order to show themselves to the people and to receive tributes. In July 1575, Queen Elizabeth I visited Kenilworth Castle a few miles north of Stratford. Kenilworth was the home of the Earl of Leicester. He was an important nobleman who, it is now thought, was trying to persuade the queen to marry him. Leicester provided the queen and her court with three weeks of entertainment. This included firework

An 18th century copy of John Scottowe's drawing shows Richard Tarlton, the player and clown, who died in 1588.

displays, hunting, **bearbaiting**, plays, and **pageants**. Many of these took place outdoors in the woods and by the lake at the castle. There was a comic country wedding for the queen to enjoy and a magnificent water pageant. Robert Langham, a court official who was present, described the events of the queen's visit to Kenilworth in a mock-serious letter a year later. Here he writes about an actor in the pageant.

> Harry Goldingham was to represent Arion upon the Dolphin's back, but finding his voice to be very hoarse and unpleasant, he tears off his disguise and swears he was none of Arion, not he, but honest Harry Goldingham: which blunt discovery pleased the Queen better than if it had gone through the right way.

In 1575, Shakespeare was 11 years old. It is possible that he, with many others, may have gone to the castle grounds to watch the festivities.

Great noblemen, such as the Earl of Leicester, had a tradition of employing groups of actors to provide entertainment for the household and its visitors. Shakespeare himself may have worked with such a company in Lancashire as a young man. When they were not performing for their employers or traveling between London and the country estates their employers owned, the companies performed in other towns and villages. Stratford had many visits from acting companies during the 1500s. In fact, the Earl of Leicester's Men played in the **Guild** Hall in Stratford in 1573 when John Shakespeare was an **alderman** and William was nine years old. Was he taken by his father to see them? Was this the beginning of the great writer?

Queen Elizabeth I also had her company of actors. In 1583, the courtier responsible for performances, the **Lord Chamberlain,** who at that time was Sir Francis Walsingham, instructed his assistant, the **Master of the Revels,** to put together a company of players. This company was made up of the best men from the other companies. The Queen's Men not only performed for the queen, they were also under her protection and were a privileged group. Their links with the queen were sometimes confusing. There is a story that when the Queen's Men were playing in Norfolk, the playgoers began to laugh when the company's clown, Richard Tarlton, stuck his head around the curtain and probably made a funny face. An officer of the law started to reprimand the audience. Their laughter was showing a lack of respect for the uniforms of the queen that the actors were wearing.

This story shows the ambivalence about plays and playing that has always been at the heart of the theater profession. Drama is both an energetic overturning of expectations and a means of displaying power and authority. Are plays carefully controlled expressions of religious or political power? Are players merely servants of the state, or are they carnivals of the human spirit? In the rise of the playing companies during the 1500s, and in William Shakespeare's participation in that rise, these questions were never far from the surface.

4
The Rise of the Playing Companies

Throughout the 1500s, plays were part of the ideas and growing unrest caused by rapid social, political, and religious changes. Rulers used drama to show their power, but they also banned plays and controlled players. For example, the **mystery cycles** were suppressed. It was felt that as products of **Catholicism** they could be a focus for unrest. This was at a time when Catholic sympathizers were seen as the state's enemies. Cities, such as Coventry, Lincoln, and Norwich, had been the home of the great mystery cycles. By the 1540s, they were centers for troupes of players who continued to travel around the country. They were part of an increasingly restless population that the government took steps to control. In May 1545, King Henry VIII proclaimed that not only "ruffians and vagabonds," but also those "common players" to be found on the south bank of the Thames River were to be forced into the navy.

There were increasingly harsh laws against uncontrolled plays throughout the 1550s. Many players risked imprisonment or worse if they staged performances that increased political and religious tension. Playing required a license. Companies attached to **guilds** or towns could not survive.

Rogues, Vagabonds, and Sturdy Beggars

The attempt to control players by making them the servants of noblemen reached its climax in the Act for the Punishment of Rogues, Vagabonds, and Sturdy Beggars of 1572. This Act was intended to prevent anyone arrested as a vagrant or beggar from claiming that they were players to avoid punishment. It kept companies of players from wandering from town to town or from one great house to another in search of an audience. The Act stated, in the legal language of the time, that

> all idle persons goinge aboute in any Countrie, either begginge, or usinge any subtile Crafte or unlawfull Games and Playes. . . all Fencers Bearwardes common Players of Enterludes [plays] and Minstrels wandringe abroad (other than Players of Enterludes belonginge to any Baron of this Realme, or any other honourable Personage of greater Degree. . .) shalbe taken adjudged and deemed as Rogues Vagabondes and Sturdie Beggers, and shall suffer such Paine and Punishment as in the saide Acte is in that behalfe appointed. . .

Other legislation tightened the link between players and their **patron**. The patron was the lord of whose household they were a part. Plays were subject to censorship. The texts had to be approved by officials of the church and state before they could be performed. The patron had to take some of the responsibility when the plays were considered unacceptable. Finally, the patron needed royal permission for his players. Queen Elizabeth never forgot that players were powerful weapons in the hands of traitorous noblemen. Players might stir up dangerous unrest throughout the towns and villages of England.

LEICESTER'S MEN

In 1574, two years after the Act for the Punishment of Rogues, Vagabonds, and Sturdy Beggars, a company of players wanted to have their situation secured. The Earl of Leicester, one of the most powerful men in England, had kept a company of players for many years. Now they wrote and asked if he would

> vouchsafe to retain us as your household servants . . . not that we
> mean to crave any further stipend or benefit at your lordship's hand
> but your liveries as we have had, and also your Honour's licence to
> certify that we are your household servants when we shall have
> occasion to travel among our friends as we do usually once a year and
> as other nobleman's players do and have done in times past.

Shortly after, the Earl of Leicester's Men received the
royal license. It is worth quoting at length, because it
lays down the rules for the development of the theater
in which Shakespeare was to flourish.

Five named players—James Burbage, John Perkyn,
John Laneham, William Johnson, and Robert
Wilson—were given permission

> to use, exercise and occupy the art and faculty of playing comedies,
> tragedies interludes stage plays and such other like . . . as well within
> our City of London and liberties of the same as also within the liberties
> and freedoms of any of our cities towns boroughs etc as without the
> same . . . provided the said comedies [etc] must be seen by the **Master
> of our Revels** . . . before seen and allowed and that the same be not
> published or shewen in the time of common prayer or in the time of
> great and common plague in our said city of London.

The letter and the license give a number of important
indications about the development of players'
companies. First, they were self-supporting. They
looked to their patron for both support and influence
at court, but otherwise they took financial
responsibility and shared the profits among
themselves. Second, they went on tour at least for
some weeks each year. Third, they had a range of plays
to perform, but the plays had to be approved by an
officer of the queen. Fourth, the license covered each
player separately. A player could set up alone, hire

other actors, and travel independently, as long as he obeyed the terms of the license. And fifth, they could play anywhere and at any time, except during church service times and outbreaks of the **plague**.

This license had two major implications for the Shakespearean theater. Daily performances meant they needed a place of their own in which to play. But the royal permission to play in London, as well as in the areas outside the control of city authorities called the **Liberties**, led to constant controversies. There were those who thought plays were a risk to health, due to spreading the plague, and a risk to morality, due to spreading treason, lust, or general disorder. The stage was set for the creation of theaters, such as The Globe. The stage was also set for the battle with the **Puritans**. The Puritans eventually won, and the theaters were closed in 1642.

STRATFORD AND LONDON

William Shakespeare may have been living in Lancashire in 1581. If he is the William Shakeshafte referred to in the will of Alexander Hoghton and afterward taken under the wing of Sir Thomas Hesketh, then he was one of a company of actors and musicians. It is possible that after Alexander Hoghton's death, Hesketh placed Shakespeare with another acting company, Lord Strange's Men. Or Shakespeare may have returned to Stratford during the summer of 1582.

Certainly by 1582, William's father, John Shakespeare, was in financial difficulty. In the years after 1578 he began to borrow money on the security of his wife's estate. In November 1582, William married Anne Hathaway, who was pregnant with their first child. Twins were born in 1585. With his brothers able to continue the gloving business, William may have begun to consider his options.

London, then as it is now, was the place to be. If William had links with powerful families, he could pick them up again in the city. If he wanted to pursue a career as a writer or player, London was where the theaters were. If he went to London, he could provide the family business with important trade contacts.

THE QUEEN'S MEN

During the 1570s a number of companies' players followed a similar pattern to Leicester's Men. The Earl of Essex's, Oxford's, Pembroke's, Warwick's, and Derby's Men toured the country in the summer, perhaps on their way to or from their patrons' country houses. Then they found a place to perform in London for the rest of the year.

We know that a company known as the Queen's Men played in Stratford in the summer of 1569 when John Shakespeare was **bailiff** and William was just five years old. But that company seems to have disbanded until 1583. The Queen's Men were reestablished when Sir Francis Walsingham, as **Lord Chamberlain** responsible for court entertainments, requested Sir Edmund Tilney, **Master of the Revels,** to choose twelve accomplished players and create the Queen's Men.

This company was different from the others in at least three ways. First, the players do not appear to have been **sharers** and were not really a business partnership. Second, they agreed only to perform as the Queen's Men. Unlike other players they could not perform on their own or join other companies. Third, they were allowed to play in the city of London without interference from the city authorities.

The Queen's Men were the most important company for the next five years. They included three of the founding players of Leicester's Men, Laneham, Wilson, and Johnson, and one of their clowns, Richard Tarlton. Tarlton was one of the most famous performers of his day. The Queen's Men toured like other companies. In the summer of 1587, they were at Thame in Oxfordshire when one of their players, William Knell, was killed in a fight. Knell was famous in serious roles. His death must have been a blow to the company. The Queen's Men were also in Stratford during that summer, though it is impossible to say whether this was before or after the death of Knell.

Some scholars have suggested that young William Shakespeare may have joined the Queen's Men at this point, not to take on Knell's roles, but to make up the numbers of a depleted company. If he had already acted with Lord Hoghton's company of players in Lancashire, then perhaps he was experienced enough to be a Queen's Men player. Certainly some of Shakespeare's later plays are reworkings of plays that were in the Queen's Men's repertoire. Maybe this is when he learned them.

Whether or not the Queen's Men included the 23-year-old William Shakespeare among their numbers when they returned to London in autumn of 1587, their glory days were soon over. Much of their success seems to have been built on the antics of their famous clown, Richard Tarlton. After Tarlton's death in September 1588, the popularity of the Queen's Men quickly declined. Many of the players transferred to other companies.

JOHN HEMINGES

The records suggest that it was common for groups of players to transfer their allegiance together. The case of John Heminges illustrates this. It may give an insight into what could have happened to William Shakespeare if he was with the Queen's Men from 1587.

On March 10, 1588, Heminges married Rebecca, the widow of the murdered William Knell. This suggests that Heminges, too, was associated with the Queen's Men. By 1593 he was a member of another company, Lord Strange's Men. A year later he was a founder, along with William Shakespeare, of the Lord Chamberlain's Men. John Heminges and William Shakespeare continued their association until Shakespeare's death in 1616 and beyond. Heminges and Henry Condell, another player with Lord Strange's Men, edited and published the collected edition of Shakespeare's plays in 1623.

Indeed, with Lord Strange's Men, scholars are on firmer ground for signs of Shakespeare. There is strong evidence that he was associated with this company beginning in 1589. Maybe he joined them at the same time as other former Queen's Men. However, some scholars think that he was with Lord Strange's Men from about 1582 and spent only short periods of time in Stratford.

LORD STRANGE'S MEN

Ferdinando, Lord Strange, was the eldest son of the fourth Earl of Derby, another of the great Lancashire **Catholic** families. Lord Strange kept a company of players throughout the 1580s, but they joined with the Admiral's Men. The arrival of actor Edward Alleyn into the company in 1589 made them famous.

Alleyn was one of the greatest players of the Elizabethan stage. He was two years younger than Shakespeare. By the time Alleyn was in his mid-twenties, he was famous for his ability to play big and energetic roles, especially the roles in the plays of Christopher Marlowe.

CHRISTOPHER MARLOWE AND THE UNIVERSITY WITS

Playwriting was being done by two distinct groups at this time. Many players produced comedies, which were often geared to the tastes of their audience. Other plays were written by university men. Some were schoolmasters writing for their pupils according to the educational principles of the day. In 1527 the boys of St. Paul's School in London performed the Latin comedy *Menaechmi* written by Plautus. By the 1550s, Nicholas Udall, headmaster of Eton School, had written *Ralph Roister Doister*, a comedy that successfully combines Latin classic plays with energetic English language and characterization. Other writers educated at Cambridge or Oxford Universities used the English language to write **tragedies**, again often following Latin classics, for performances at the universities or at the royal court.

Edward Alleyn (1566–1626), was one of the greatest actors of his day. This portrait hangs in Dulwich College, London, the school he founded in 1616.

By the 1580s, university educated writers were also providing plays for the companies. Some were delicate comedies, full of fantasy and the supernatural with serious undercurrents. For example, John Lyly's *Campaspe* of 1584 is described as "a tragical comedie." The mixture of styles is even more pronounced in George Peele's *The Old Wives' Tale* (1591). Lyly and Peele wrote for highly professional companies of **boy players**. But another university man, Robert Greene, made his mark with the adult companies, perhaps even the Queen's Men and Lord Strange's Men. He wrote plays, such as *James the Fourth* about Scottish courtly intrigue, and *Friar Bacon and Friar Bungay,* which mixes clowning and romance in ways that will be seen again later in Shakespeare's plays.

Without a doubt the greatest of the university-educated playwrights was Christopher Marlowe. Marlowe was a rebel. His plays burn with anger, wit, irreverence, and defiance like none before him. In *Tamburlaine,* written about 1587, he paints a sweeping picture of a world conqueror achieving greatness before he falls like a burned-out rocket. *Doctor Faustus,* written about 1587, is about a pact with the devil that leads to loss of life and soul. *The Jew of Malta,* written about 1589, is a portrait of all-consuming evil succumbing not to goodness, but to greater, political cunning.

Marlowe's plays focus on a great man rising above and conquering the world around him using fire, sword, or wickedness before drowning in the seas of blood he created. Marlowe's plays have the energy of the battles between good and evil that are found in the religious plays of the **mystery cycles.** But goodness has almost disappeared from Marlowe's world of cunning politicians, wily devils, and scheming courtiers. The central characters are much larger than life and need an exceptional player to bring them off. In Edward Alleyn, Lord Strange's Men found just the right actor.

Marlowe's plays were a huge and scandalous success. He showed how the public theaters could tackle big themes with intelligence, flair, and showmanship. His plays were noisy, energetic spectacles that explored complex political and moral issues. If Shakespeare was now acting with Lord Strange's Men and establishing himself as a writer, he would be learning his craft from these plays.

5
THE ONELY SHAKE-SCENE IN A COUNTREY

However he got there, whether with the Queen's Men or Lord Strange's Men, William Shakespeare was part of the London theater scene by 1592. By then, he was almost certainly engaged with Lord Strange's Men and making a name for himself as a player and playwright. But he was making enemies as well.

In September 1592, a pamphlet appeared. It was said to have been written on the deathbed of the playwright Robert Greene. The pamphlet, *Greene's Groatsworth of Wit,* makes a number of accusations against another writer who had been an acquaintance, if not a friend. The other writer had failed to help Greene in his time of need.

> there is an upstart Crow, beautified with our feathers, that with his Tygers hart wrapt in a Players hyde, supposes he is as well able to bombast out a blank verse as the best of you: and beeing an absolute *Johannes fac totum,* is in his owne conceit the onely Shake-scene in a countrey... O that I might intreat your rare wits to be imploied in more profitable courses... I knowe the best husband of you will never prove a Usurer and the kindest of them all will never prove a kind nurse...

Whoever wrote this pamphlet was attacking Shakespeare. He parodies a line from one of Shakespeare's earliest plays, *The True Tragedy of Richard, Duke of York, and the Death of Good King Henry the Sixth. . .,* known today as *Henry VI Part 3.* In the play, the Duke of York refers to Queen Margaret as a "tiger's heart wrapped in a woman's hide." And "Shake-scene" clinches it. Who else could this be but Shakespeare?

The attack gives more information that may help draw a picture of Shakespeare as his contemporaries saw him in 1592. First, the author directs his warnings about "Shake-scene" to writers like himself, who were university educated men. They had written plays for the boy companies, the Queen's Men, and Lord Strange's Men. But here was a newcomer, "an upstart Crow," outdoing them at their own craft. He was a player turned playwright: *Johannes fac totum,* is Latin for "Jack of all trades"—someone who is skilled in many areas.

Shakespeare's success was condemning the established writers to poverty. Presumably, Shakespeare's radical experiments had made Greene's, Lyly's, and Peele's plays no longer fashionable. The author of the pamphlet also accuses "Shake-scene" of arrogance: "in his owne conceit the onely Shake-scene in a countrey." Finally, he refers to him as a usurer, a moneylender, who would not help Greene in his distress, but who hoards his money for his own purposes.

The attack may be a case of sour grapes, but a realistic picture emerges that is repeated throughout Shakespeare's life. By the early 1580s, his father, John Shakespeare, had fallen on hard times. All merchants needed to be able to borrow and lend money at different times, and John Shakespeare did both. At times he even lived in fear of being arrested for debt. But by 1596, he is referred to as a man of wealth. William must have used his success as a player, who is better paid than a playwright, to remake the family fortune, and acquire wealth and property.

THE FIRST PLAYS

It is not known for sure when Shakespeare began to write plays. Some scholars think that none of the plays later collected into the **Folio** of 1623 was written before 1590. Others would date the earliest plays to 1587 or 1588. Four pieces of evidence support the earlier dates.

1. The attack in *Greene's Groatsworth of Wit* shows a man already successful and well-known. Surely this must be built on more than two years' worth of play-writing!

2. In 1614, Shakespeare's great play-writing contemporary, Ben Jonson, in his play *Bartholomew Fair*, refers to Shakespeare's *Titus Andronicus* as having been written "some twenty-five or thirty years" earlier. This would date it to between 1584 and 1589. A date of 1584 seems too early, because the grasp of dramatic technique is too assured for a 20-year-old writer. A date of 1589 or a little earlier would be quite possible.

3. The title page of the printed edition of *Titus Andronicus* (1594) tells us that it had already been performed by three companies. The closure of the theaters throughout most of 1593 meant that companies were touring. It appears that a group of Lord Strange's Men separated from the main company and toured as the Earl of Pembroke's Men. By September 1593, they were bankrupt and sold some plays, either to printers or to other companies. *Titus Andronicus* was one of these. Presumably, Pembroke's Men took with them a well-established play that was already in their repertoire when they separated from Lord Strange's Men. They sold it to another company to help pay off their debts.

4. In the early play, *The Two Gentlemen of Verona,* the comic character, Launce, has a dog. It is possible that the role was played by or written for the great clown, Richard Tarlton, who had a performing dog. Tarlton died in 1588. No other known clown at the time had a performing dog. The play seems to have not been performed again during Shakespeare's lifetime. Did the play die with Tarlton? If so, it may have been written for him and the Queen's Men in or before 1588.

The Two Gentlemen of Verona shifts the gentle love-comedies of John Lyly from the boys' companies into the world of adult players and raises the tension and emotional range. Proteus and Valentine are good friends. Proteus is loved by Julia. When Valentine leaves Verona for Milan, another Italian town, Proteus decides to follow him. His friendship for Valentine is greater than his love for Julia. But in Milan, both young men fall in love with the same woman, Silvia. Towards the end of the play, Proteus rescues Silvia, who has been captured by outlaws. But she is still not safe because Proteus threatens to rape her. Fortunately, Valentine is hiding nearby, sees what his former friend is trying to do, and stops him. Proteus has been a poor friend to Valentine, betrayed Julia's love, and threatened an innocent woman. Good friendship and true love turn bad. Even the closest relationships are fragile. The play resolves itself quickly and not altogether convincingly. Valentine forgives Proteus, who hands over Silvia. A pageboy turns out to be Julia in disguise. She is reunited with Proteus, and all ends more happily than Proteus's behavior perhaps deserves.

Even in such an early play, many typically Shakespearean themes are present. Throughout his career, he tracked the intricate paths of love and friendship, made great use of disguise, and allowed a comic subplot to mirror and illuminate the moral and psychological worlds of the characters. Although rarely performed, *The Two Gentlemen of Verona* has funny scenes. The verse in which the lovers speak is full of wit and insight. Above all, Shakespeare has already learned to show, and not just tell, his stories.

The Taming of the Shrew is almost certainly another very early play. *The Two Gentlemen of Verona* explored the **rhetoric** of friendship, using balanced and repetitive verse to show the shifting feelings of the lovers. *The Taming of the Shrew* examines the power games below the surface of love and marriage. Already the gap between truth and appearance is opening. The suspicion that words may not mean what they say is taking hold.

The plot is complex. Three plots intertwine and illuminate one other. First, as a frame to the play, the drunken Christopher Sly is tricked into thinking he is a lord for whom a play is to be performed. That play has two layers. One is the wooing of the shrewish, bad-tempered, foul-mouthed Katherine by Petruccio, who is on the lookout for a rich wife. The second layer is the attempts of Lucentio, Gremio, and Hortensio to marry Katherine's sister, Bianca. The play has stock characters and scenes that are reminders of the Italian *Commedia* tradition. The play is a hilarious **farce**. But there is a serious undercurrent. Bianca's suitors see wooing as a business venture, although they protest that they love her. Petruccio treats the wooing of

Katherine like a business deal, but he seems to transform her into a loving wife.

Near the end of the play, the men bet on which woman will be the most obedient wife. To everyone's surprise, Katherine wins. She makes a long speech telling women that husbands should be the lords and masters of their wives.

> Thy husband is thy lord, thy life, thy keeper,
> Thy head, thy sovereign, one that cares for thee. . .
> And craves no other tribute at thy hands
> But love, fair looks, and true obedience. . .
> Such duty as the subject owes the prince,
> Even such a woman oweth to her husband, . .'
>
> *The Taming of the Shrew*, Act 5 Scene 2, lines 151–152, 157–158, 160–161

This speech might appear preposterous, even offensive, today, but when performed it can give a very different impression than that of the printed page.

Katherine is simply stating the beliefs of her day, and the speech can be played that way. But actresses playing Katherine today often make other choices. After the speech, Petruccio seems surprised. He says, "Why, there's a wench!" Perhaps Katherine has decided to be like her husband, Petruccio, and subvert expectations, shock those around her, and be a free spirit. Or maybe Katherine accepts that this is the public role of a wife, but in private things can be very different. Husbands and wives rely on one another in ways the world never sees. They become a team. Or maybe Katherine knows that Petruccio has bet on her obedience, and she plays the game with him. Once more, it is the two of them against the world.

The number of choices available to an actor show that nothing can be taken at face value in a Shakespeare play. There is always a gap between appearance and reality. The Shakespearean truth is more likely to be found between many options, rather than fixed with clear certainty.

With his next two plays, written probably in 1590–1591, Shakespeare broke new ground. He explored the history of England as it collapsed into civil war under King Henry VI in the middle of the 15th century. *The First Part of the Contention of the Two Famous Houses of York and Lancaster with the Death of the Good Duke Humphrey* is known in most editions as *Henry VI Part 2*, and here as *The Contention*. It looks at the ten years between 1445 and 1455 as a weak king struggled unsuccessfully against his nobles. Richard, Duke of York, tries to overthrow Henry by manipulating a peasant rebellion led by Jack Cade. As the play closes, Richard seems about to take the throne.

The True Tragedy of Richard, Duke of York and the Death of Good King Henry the Sixth (Henry VI Part 3) picks up the story. Richard is killed early in the story. The play focuses on his sons' struggle with Queen Margaret, Henry's wife, for control of the country. *The True Tragedy* ends with Henry and his son murdered by the Yorkists; with Richard's son, Edward, Earl of March, on the throne as Edward IV; and another son, Richard, Duke of Gloucester, preparing his own murderous way to the throne.

Shakespeare relied extensively on Raphael Holinshed's *Chronicles*, a history of the time printed in 1587. But

Shakespeare's plays skillfully manipulate history to reveal political and personal ambitions on the battlefields of England. They are bold, sweeping epics where armies march and countermarch, murders are committed and avenged, and much blood is spilled.

There are also many complex characterizations. The saintly Henry VI is shocked by the civil war around him. Richard of Gloucester schemes. The Earl of Warwick plays power politics. There are also many small but beautifully crafted roles of George, Duke of Clarence, the brother of Edward and Richard; Lady Grey, who will marry King Edward; a soldier who has killed his son; and another soldier who has killed his father. Shakespeare paints a picture in which battles between the rival noble houses of Lancaster and York tear England apart from top to bottom. At the end, Margaret is banished to France and King Edward proclaims a time of peace, but the very last line of the play sounds a note of foreboding.

> For here, I hope, begins our lasting joy.

This speech gives insight into Richard of Gloucester's ambitions.

> Henry and his sons are gone; thou, Clarence, art next;
> And one by one I will dispatch the rest,
> Counting myself but bad till I be best.
>
> *The True Tragedy. . .,* Act 5 Scene 6, lines 90–92

Before Shakespeare completed his account of the lives of Henry VI, Edward IV, and Richard III, he worked on *Titus Andronicus*. It was written around 1591 or a little earlier, when gory tales of revenge with horror piling on horror were in fashion. *Titus Andronicus* translates Latin classic plays of this kind into a thoroughly English idiom. Shakespeare's main model was the Roman dramatist Seneca. Many of Seneca's tragedies were being translated during Shakespeare's time. They are as full of highly theatrical revenge killings as any Hollywood gangster movie and as terrifying as any horror movie. On the page, the action may seem silly, but when performed, audiences can still be moved to terror and pity.

In *Titus Andronicus,* the language is formal and has the effect of distancing the events from the onlooker. Tamora, Queen of the Goths, avenges her son's death by enabling her other sons, Demetrius and Chiron, to rape her captor Titus's daughter, Lavinia. They also cut off Lavinia's hands and pull out her tongue to prevent her from telling who did it. Titus is tricked into cutting off his hand in order, as he thinks, to save his own sons' lives. Then Titus and his brother Marcus kill the rapists, cook them, and serve them up in a pie to be eaten by their mother. Titus kills Lavinia to remove her shame and then kills Tamora herself. Tamora's husband kills Titus and then is killed by Titus's last remaining son, Lucius. In ancient Greek tragedy, the **chorus** wore masks with wide open eyes so that they could not turn away from the terrifying scenes they were called on to witness. So it is that Shakespeare's formal language also distances the audience from the events, while keeping the audience open-eyed to wonder at the blood being spilled and to pity the waste of so much life.

In early 1592, Shakespeare returned to English history. He wrote a play now generally referred to as *Henry VI Part 1* in which the events leading up to the struggles of *The Contention. . .* and *The True Tragedy (Henry*

VI Parts 2 and 3) are recounted. Many scholars think Shakespeare was not solely responsible for the play, but that he collaborated with at least two other authors. This was a common practice in the Elizabethan theater.

Henry VI Part 1 shows how the unity of England fell apart after the death of King Henry V. Throughout the play, Shakespeare and his collaborators use dramatic techniques to pull widely spaced historical events into a single scene. The play opens, for example, with nobles bickering at King Henry's funeral while messengers arrive to tell of the loss of the lands in France. The losses, in fact, took place over several years. It goes on to tell of the growth of the two factions of the white rose—York—and the red rose—Lancaster—as symbolized by a scene in a garden, act 2 scene 4, probably written by Shakespeare. In this scene, the opposing forces choose roses to advertise their allegiance. The Earl of Warwick draws back the veil of history.

> this brawl today,
> Grown to this faction in the Temple garden,
> Shall send, between the red rose and the white,
> A thousand souls to death and deadly night
>
> *Henry VI Part 1, Act 2 Scene 4, lines 124–127*

The play ends with wars in France. The French are portrayed as treacherous. Their hero, Joan of Arc, is portrayed as a witch. But the wars allow a hero, Lord Talbot, to emerge before he and his son are betrayed by the squabbling Yorkists and Lancastrians. Deprived of troops to support them, Lord Talbot and his son die valiantly, but uselessly.

If *Henry VI Part 1* establishes the fighting that was to lead to civil war, then *Richard III,* written probably a few months later towards the end of 1592, brings it all to a bloody conclusion.

In the earlier plays about Henry VI and the Wars of the Roses, Shakespeare began to twist history to create dramatic effects. In this play, he does not let history stand in the way of a good story. The sources he used were themselves highly biased accounts written by supporters of Henry VII and the **Tudors** who had defeated Richard. Shakespeare was unaware of this, but even he changed the information and the time frame to focus attention on Richard's climb to the throne.

Richard got to the throne through a process of lying, cheating, manipulating, and murdering his opponents and his friends. And yet, like so many dramatic portraits of evil, this Richard is mesmerizing. He plays with the other characters and with the audience like a snake with a rabbit. He is energetic and witty and always a step ahead of the rest, until his conscience catches up with him. Then he falls to what Shakespeare invites us to see as the force of good. That good force is Henry Richmond, who becomes Henry VII, Queen Elizabeth's grandfather.

Although *Richard III* may not be historically accurate, Shakespeare does create his first full-blooded villain to stand alongside the overreaching characters of the playwright Christopher Marlowe. Marlowe's Jew of Malta, named Barabas, and Shakespeare's King Richard both proclaim themselves as followers of the Italian analyzer of political power games, Niccoló Machiavelli. Modern scholarship shows that

Machiavelli's work is a complex and not necessarily approving picture of how rulers can gain power and stay in control. But in the English popular imagination at the end of the 1500s, *Machiavelli* was a byword for evil. When in *The True Tragedy. . .* Shakespeare has Richard say that he will "set the murderous Machiavel to school" (act 3 scene 2), he makes it clear that this man will stop at nothing to gain power and will cheat and murder his way to the throne.

These early plays lay out a number of themes that Shakespeare developed throughout his working life. In the comedies *The Two Gentlemen of Verona* and *The Taming of the Shrew,* he explores ideas of friendship, love, and marriage and shows how relationships shift and change when under pressure. He also experiments with ways of showing the complexity of human beings. Few of his characters, even in these early plays, are simple or act from unmixed motives.

As Shakespeare's skill develops, he seems to invent the history play form. The gap between appearance and reality widens. The undoing of politicians, such as the Duke of Somerset in *The True Tragedy. . .* or the revengers Tamora and Titus Andronicus, reaches a climax in Richard III's lethal maneuvering. The language of the plays becomes simpler and more direct. At the same time, the language carries richer and more telling ambiguity. In a world where no one ever quite means what they say and actions are two-edged swords, the pretense of the playhouse has become the place to examine human life.

THE PLAYHOUSES

Plays need playing places. The requirements of being able to hear and see imply either a raised stage or sloped floor, as in ancient Greek and Roman theaters. A theater also needs a way to focus the player's voice, while blocking out unnecessary noise. The medieval plays associated with **Corpus Christi** were performed either on and around carts or on specially built stages. For other occasions, wooden stages, called scaffolds, might be erected inside churches, market halls, the great halls of houses, university colleges and schools, or in the open air.

Such stages were temporary affairs. For example, between 1546 and about 1638, Queens' College, Cambridge, had a scaffold made of 500 pieces of timber. It was built once a year in the hall, but kept in storage the rest of the year. Inns used for performances by touring companies in London or around the country may have required similar temporary arrangements. A room would be cleared of furniture, or a scaffold would be built in the courtyard.

The first specially built public playhouse opened in Great Yarmouth in about 1538. The first playhouse in London was the Red Lion, built in 1567 by a grocer named John Brayne. The name of this playhouse has led people to think it was an inn, but this is not the case. Recent legal documents show that it was designed and built by Brayne in the courtyard of a farmhouse located just outside the Aldgate on what is now Whitechapel High Street.

Little is known about the Red Lion, but more is known about the playhouse built by James Burbage,

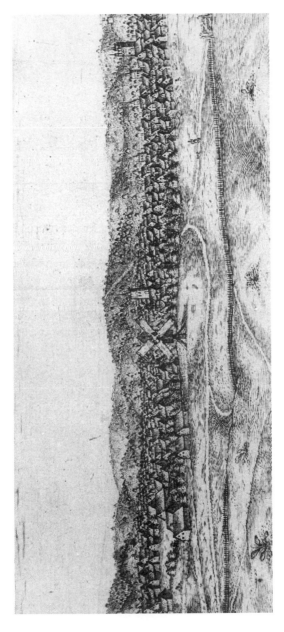

This engraved illustration of London, as viewed from the north in about 1597, shows a building with a flag. This may be The Theatre, built by James Burbage in 1576. The engraving is in the Utrecht University Library, Holland.

who was Brayne's brother-in-law. Burbage was a leader of Leicester's Men and the father of Richard Burbage, Shakespeare's famous fellow player.

Burbage's playhouse was called The Theatre. It was built in 1576 on a site west of what is now Shoreditch High Street, north of Holywell Lane. A year later another playhouse, The Curtain, was built, probably by Henry Lanman. It was on the other side of Holywell Lane.

The building of The Theatre was the result of the new situation for companies, such as Leicester's Men. Their license allowed them to perform daily, if not in the city, then in its **Liberties**, such as Shoreditch, just outside the city walls. Temporary arrangements in other buildings hardly allowed regular arrangements to be made. But there were other implications.

1. The companies were, with the exception of the Queen's Men, business ventures. In 1599, it cost one penny to stand to watch a play at The Curtain. It cost another penny to have a seat and still another penny for a seat with a cushion and a good view. Popular players could earn good money. The entrepreneurs who laid out the initial capital and took the financial risks could make a fortune.

2. Playhouses were used by more than one company. The Theatre may have been a home for Leicester's Men, but at least six other companies played there, including Shakespeare's companies, Lord Strange's Men, and Lord Chamberlain's Men. It is likely that the early plays of Shakespeare and Christopher Marlowe had their first London performances on the stage of The Theatre.

3. The difference between The Theatre and The Curtain shows that the London theater scene in Shakespeare's time was varied. The Theatre probably attracted a wealthier, more serious playgoer than The Curtain, which became famous for its rowdy audiences, bawdy shows, and crowd-pleasing spectacles.

4. The Theatre and The Curtain, like the Red Lion and most other later London playhouses, were located just outside the city walls. There was constant tension between the city authorities and the playing companies because the companies were looked on with some suspicion as spreaders of **plague**, crime, immorality, and rebellion. Unfavorable pleasures were offered in the Liberties. Playhouses stood side-by-side with **bearbaiting, bullbaiting,** and **brothels**. Playhouse owners earned money from these entertainments, too.

At the end of Chapter 3, were these questions: Are plays carefully controlled expressions of religious or political power? Are players merely servants of the state, or are they carnivals of the human spirit? As the playing companies and their playhouses developed during the 1500s, these questions became more important. The companies were controlled by royal license and linked to noble **patrons**. They were expected to be available to perform at court or at the houses of their patrons to add to the magnificent display that established power in the land. At the same time, the playhouses were in the Liberties, on the margins of the city. Players were both at the center and on the margins of society. But the energy of their work brought anarchy to the forefront. It is not coincidental that players were called to court to perform at the **Lord of Misrule** and Carnival, which come after

Christmas and before the beginning of Lent.

In this sense the **Liberties** were the natural home of the players. Into those marginal places, north of the city walls and south of the river, Elizabethan society banished all its fears. Death was found in the hospitals, places of execution, and cemeteries. Sex was found in the **brothels.** The animal instincts and pleasures were found in the **bullbaiting, bearbaiting,** and **cockfighting.** Here, too, were the players, whose stories disturb, overturn, and lay bare the hidden motives of men and women. In the playhouses of the Liberties, these fears could be addressed and, if not tamed, then controlled and allowed back in through the city gates. In Shakespeare's early plays, this ambivalence of order and chaos was already being held to the light.

6

PLAGUE, POEMS, AND PATRONS

London stank. Its rivers were thick with garbage. Its rapidly growing population walked along streets made slippery by sewage. Wherever two or three families gathered together, there was likely to be a dunghill. Vegetable plots were watered from drainage ditches. The houses, alive with rats, fleas, and lice, were breeding grounds of disease. In the overcrowded streets, disease spread like wildfire. The people lived in fear of **plague.**

Bubonic plague had been a constant threat in England since 1348–1350, the years of the Black Death. The Black Death wiped out about 40 million people, about 25 percent of the population of Europe. During the 16th and 17th centuries, hardly a year went by without an outbreak of plague in London and elsewhere in the country. There was a severe outbreak in Stratford in 1564, the year Shakespeare was born.

Bubonic plague was the most feared of all epidemic diseases. It is spread by the bite of parasitic insects that normally live on rats. The heat of summer and the filthy conditions of the towns led to outbreaks of the disease as rats and their parasites bred uncontrollably. Anyone infected developed a headache and a general sense of tiredness. Soon they began to vomit and their joints ached. Within hours the groin and the areas under the arm or on the side of the neck began to swell. The patient ran a temperature. The swellings, called buboes—hence the name bubonic plague— increased to the size of a chicken's egg. The pulse raced and breathing became more difficult. Within about four days, the patient turned purple as his or her lungs failed. Death put an end to the intense suffering. The disease was a fast but painful killer.

Because the cause of the **plague** was not known, no measures could be taken to effect a cure. Town and city authorities tried their best by banning gatherings that might spread the infection. This included a ban on performances at playhouses. Those who could get out of the cities, heavy with the stench of death and decay, and into the country, often took the infection with them.

In June 1592, with the plague threatening once more, London authorities, already alarmed by a riot of **apprentices** a few days earlier, proclaimed that no plays could be performed, not even in the **Liberties**, because the crowds gathering there might spread the disease. This might have been an excuse to reduce the threat of disturbance, as London was suffering the effects of economic failure and famine. But it prevented the players from earning a living. The prohibition was reaffirmed in January 1593. The playhouses remained closed for the rest of that year.

Players went out on the road again, including a group from Lord Strange's Men, who toured during the summer of 1593. They probably took some of Shakespeare's plays with them. It is possible that Shakespeare joined them, but his name does not appear on the license permitting the company to play as the Earl of Pembroke's Men. The bankruptcy of the rest of the company, which was forced to sell personal effects and its stock of plays that same autumn, does not seem to have affected Shakespeare. In 1592 he was probably living in a northern area of the city badly hit by plague. Maybe he took this opportunity to return home to Stratford and explore other writing options.

Doctor Samuel Johnson, compiling his famous *Dictionary of the English Language* published in 1755, defined a person who makes dictionaries as "a harmless drudge." He could also have been describing most playwrights of Shakespeare's time. There was money to be made in the playhouses, but it went to the owner, the players, and even the provider of food and drink, rather than to the writer. This is not altogether unfair. After all, the idea of a play text as a piece of literature to be read like a novel or a poem is a very modern idea.

If plays were printed at all during Shakespeare's lifetime, that meant they had reached the end of their useful life for a company or had been given to a printer against the company's wishes. Like the score of a piece of music, a play text only exists when it is being performed. Real meaning emerges only in the interaction among the actors and between actors and audience. The writer's role is significant. Shakespeare's contribution to the raised status of playwrights is crucial, but only as a partner. Playwrights and actors know that the text performed on the opening night is the product of collaboration. The text may change again with the experience of performance. This was probably no different for Shakespeare.

HENRY WRIOTHESLEY, EARL OF SOUTHAMPTON

To be noticed or to earn a living, a writer had to find someone who would support, protect, and, hopefully, pay him. The best way to find a supporter was to appeal to vanity and to flatter a potential **patron** by dedicating a work of art to him.

The two poems Shakespeare wrote and had printed, between the autumn of 1592 and May 1594, were dedicated to the 18-year-old Henry Wriothesley, Earl of Southampton. Southampton was a friend of the Earl of Essex, who was a great favorite of the queen. The two earls shared a desire to be brave and glorious courtiers and soldiers after the manner of one of the most famous men of the time, Sir Philip Sidney. Sir Sidney had died of wounds sustained in fighting in the Low Countries, the Netherlands, in 1586. But there were few foreign wars to fight, and their ambitions were frustrated by the older noblemen who were the queen's advisers. Full of ambition to glitter like the princes of the European courts, they were limited instead to petty intrigues and the tedium of life in the royal palaces.

VENUS AND ADONIS

There is no evidence that Shakespeare knew Southampton before he dedicated "Venus and Adonis" to him in February 1593. The letter at the start of the poem could simply be a few well-turned phrases aimed at attracting his attention. But within the dedication, an interesting phrase stands out. Shakespeare refers to the book as "the first heir of my invention." Presumably it was his first printed work, but it also perhaps indicates how little Shakespeare either rated or wanted to draw attention to the plays for which he was becoming well-known. Advertising yourself as a playwright or player was not necessarily the right way to commend yourself to a nobleman.

Among the books that a **grammar school** boy would have read were the *Metamorphoses* of Ovid, an ancient Roman author. The stories that Ovid tells concern mysterious and miraculous changes. Their constant interchange between appearance and reality would be likely to have fascinated Shakespeare. The story of Venus and Adonis takes up 75 lines of Book 10. Shakespeare expands it to 1,194 lines made up of six-line verses. In doing so, he changes the poem with disturbing effect. In Ovid's story, the handsome youth Adonis returns the love of the goddess Venus. In Shakespeare, Adonis tries to avoid her.

> She red and hot as coals of glowing fire;
> He red for shame, but frosty in desire.
>
> *Venus and Adonis*, lines 35–36

These lines already make clear the structure of the **rhetoric** in the verse. Both Venus and Adonis are "red," but she for lust, he for shame. The rhyming couplets regularly create effects that balance and draw a contrast at the same time. It gives the effect of drawing Venus and Adonis together while keeping them separate. It is one of Shakespeare's most characteristic rhetorical devices, found in his plays as well as his poems.

As the poem develops, Shakespeare draws away from Ovid's characters. Venus and Adonis become complex characters and their interplay becomes increasingly realistic. Adonis sets off on a fatal hunt to get away from Venus. She waits anxiously for news, fears the worst, finds his body, and laments his death.

> Alas, poor world, what treasure hast thou lost,
> What face remains alive that's worth the viewing?
> Whose tongue is music now? What canst thou boast

79

Of things long since, or anything ensuing?
>The flowers are sweet, their colours fresh and trim;
>But true sweet beauty lived and died with him.
Venus and Adonis, lines 1075–1080

The lovers are flesh and blood, which makes the charge of the poem all the greater. When it comes to the transformation at the end of the poem, this realism pays off. In Ovid, the dead Adonis is changed into a flower, an anemone. In Shakespeare, one real thing, a dead boy, is replaced by another real thing, the flower.

By this, the boy that by her side lay killed
Was melted like a vapour from her sight,
And in his blood that on the ground lay spilled
A purple flower sprang up, chequered with white,
>Resembling well his pale cheeks, and the blood
>Which in round drops upon their whiteness stood.
Venus and Adonis, 1165–1170

THE RAPE OF LUCRECE

Fourteen months later, in May 1594 with the playhouses reopening, a second poem, "The Rape of Lucrece," was dedicated to Southampton. The letter at the beginning of the book is more relaxed and friendly. This time it speaks of "the warrant I have of your honourable disposition." Is this asking for some positive response or a payment of money? "My duty. . . is bound to your lordship" makes it appear that some sort of relationship has opened up between them.

"The Rape of Lucrece" is also based on Ovid, but it is a tragic story of lust and rape. This is the opposite of "Venus and Adonis." In the earlier poem, the woman tries to seduce the man. In this poem, the man rapes the woman. Adonis dies hunting a boar, Lucrece kills herself. The verses have seven lines and the rhetorical effect is darker.

In "The Rape of Lucrece," Shakespeare explored the worlds of the great **tragedies** written some years later. Tarquin is a portrait of vicious lust.

> Into the chamber wickedly he stalks,
> And gazeth on her yet-unstainèd bed.
> The curtains being close, about he walks,
> Rolling his greedy eye-balls in his head.
>
> *The Rape of Lucrece,* lines 365–370

Lucrece reveals her feelings through soliloquies, which are speeches when a single actor expresses thoughts and feelings to the audience.

> Where now I have no one to blush with me,
> To cross their arms and hang their heads with mine,
> To mask their brows and hide their infamy,
> But I alone, alone must sit and pine,
> Seasoning the earth with showers of silver brine,
> Mingling my talk with tears, my grief with groans,
> Poor wasting monuments of lasting moans.
>
> *The Rape of Lucrece,* lines 792–798

LOVE'S LABOUR'S LOST

One aspect of Elizabethan poetry that modern readers can find particularly difficult is its love of elegant and complicated word play. As well as the rhetorical techniques of "Venus and Adonis," writers and readers delighted in puns, hidden messages, allusions to events, authors, and people. The poems were like complex and witty coded messages that depended on secret knowledge for full understanding. At about the same time that Shakespeare was writing the two poems, he was also working on a new play, *Love's Labour's Lost*. Unusual for Shakespeare, the plot was his own invention. Shakespeare generally borrowed basic stories from elsewhere, which he then twisted and developed to give new insights.

Love's Labour's Lost is about the King of Navarre and his three friends. They have decided to live in isolation from women and undertake academic study. Almost at once the Princess of France and three of her ladies arrive on a diplomatic mission. Predictably, the men fall in love, and there is much comic confusion as they try to hide the fact from each other. The confusions grow as the men, disguised as Russians, entertain the women. The women, in the meantime, to make fun of the men, have swapped identities.

The language of the characters is a dazzling display of verbal wit, very like the poetry Shakespeare was dedicating to the Earl of Southampton. But the play's language is limited to an expression of human life and the limitations of human life that can only be lived through witty display. First, the comic characters' attempts to use similar wit fall flat with hilarious results. Second, Costard the clown and his girlfriend Jacquenetta need no words as a substitute for love. And third, near the end of the play, a messenger, Mercadé, arrives with bad news.

It is this moment that shows most clearly the difference between poetry and a play. Mercadé's entrance from the world of pain and death reminds characters and audience alike of the limitations of wit. The impact depends on his physical presence, a silent figure among the chattering lovers and wordy fools. His language is simple and direct. It needs no display to give its message, which can hardly be spoken.

Mercadé: God save you, madam.
Princess: Welcome, Mercadé,
           But that thou interrupt's our merriment.
Mercadé: I am sorry, madam, for the news I bring
           Is heavy in my tongue. The King your father–
Princess: Dead, for my life.
Mercadé: Even so. My tale is told.
Biron: Worthies, away. The scene begins to cloud.

Love's Labour's Lost, Act 5 Scene 2, lines 709–715

THE LONDON BOOK TRADE

There are five basic steps to produce a book. First, the writer produces a text, called a manuscript. Second, a publisher accepts the text and decides to make it widely available. Third, a printer turns the text into many identical copies. Fourth, a bookseller obtains copies from the publisher and puts them on sale. Fifth and finally, readers buy the book. This modern process is almost the same way Shakespeare's poems and some of his early plays were made available to readers in Elizabethan England.

The center of the London book trade at that time was the streets around old St. Paul's Cathedral. Writers came to this area to try to find someone to publish their books. Once they found someone willing to publish, the text had to be approved by an officer of the church. The text also had to be licensed by the **Guild** of Stationers, who controlled book production. This license was given only when all agreed that the

83

publication of the book would not affect the rights of anyone else. Finally, the book was entered on the Register of the Guild. This allowed a printer to print it.

The streets around St. Paul's were full of booksellers' stalls and printers' workshops. The stalls and workshops were identified by a sign hanging outside. "Venus and Adonis" was available at the shop displaying "the signe of the Angel" and also at John Harrison's shop beneath "the sign of the White Greyhound."

Some bookshops probably specialized in certain books. Others took the books they thought would sell. But just as any printer might be approached to produce a book, any bookseller could obtain copies for his shop. On June 12, 1593, a man named Richard Stonely was looking around the bookshops. He stopped at John Harrison's and bought *the Venus & Adhonay pr Shakspear* (the Venus and Adonis by Shakespeare). He probably paid sixpence, or about 10 cents.

Venus and Adonis and *The Rape of Lucrece* were printed by John Field, a man three years older than Shakespeare. Field was also from Stratford. The two would have been at school together before Field was sent to London to be **apprenticed** into the printing trade. When Shakespeare looked for someone to produce his first printed books, he probably turned to an old friend who had begun to specialize in printing high-quality texts. For his first publications, Shakespeare was determined to have the best.

7

ENTERTAINERS AND ENTREPRENEURS

Theater is an expensive business. The great cycles of mystery plays cost a great deal to perform. By the early 1500s, demands for better staging and better actors were making the plays costly. The **pageants**, tournaments, and other entertainments by which kings and noblemen showed their power were also hugely expensive. The economics of the 16th century placed ready money into the hands of a larger group of tradesmen, farmers, merchants, and the professions. The players remained servants of the aristocracy, but beginning in the 1580s, playing companies were businesses. Of course, this met the needs of the courtiers, too. As long as they could call on the players from time to time for their own entertainments, the companies could be self-supporting.

The playing companies were in the business of making money, and there were two ways to be profitable. One was to own a playhouse or to have sole rights for providing a service. James Burbage made his money from The Theatre, and Henry Lanman made his money from The Curtain. Philip Henslowe held the lease for The Rose, a playhouse built south of the Thames River in the **Liberty** of the Clink. Henslowe's partner, John Cholmley, took over a cottage near The Rose. At the cottage, he provided refreshments for playgoers. He had the sole rights to provide food and drink.

The other way to be profitable was to manage or to be a **sharer** in a playing company. A sharer might even own the plays that were performed. James Burbage and Philip Henslowe were rival managers, one on each side of the river. In May 1591, Burbage was arguing with his players at The Theatre. This was the combined company of Lord Strange's and the Admiral's Men. The players accused Burbage of keeping back some of their share of the money. Some of the players, led by the star Edward Alleyn, walked out. They crossed the river to form the core of Henslowe's company at The Rose. They would have taken some of their repertoire of plays with them— perhaps Alleyn owned them—but, with the exception of the play *Titus Andronicus,* none of the plays appears to have been written by Shakespeare. It is possible that Richard Burbage, James's son, owned the rest of Shakespeare's plays at this time. Richard was probably linked with the ill-fated Pembroke's Men. This company's touring ended disastrously in 1593, and some of their plays were printed to raise money.

The financial arrangements at The Rose show how income was shared. Henslowe received money from Cholmley four times a year as part of the agreement for the sale of refreshments. In turn, Cholmley kept the profits from the "breade and drinke." Henslowe had paid for the construction of the theater. He also provided money for the costumes and other items for the performance. He kept meticulous account books, which give information about playhouse performances at the time. Henslowe and Cholmley shared the responsibility for finding players. They also agreed to be present at performances to keep an eye on the money. Henslowe and Cholmley equally shared half the money from the sale of tickets for gallery seats. The other half of the gallery ticket money and all the income from the sale of tickets for standing room in front of the stage was divided among the actors.

In 1592, a year after he arrived at The Rose, the actor Alleyn married Henslowe's stepdaughter Joan Woodward. They began to take a greater part in running the family business. After Alleyn's arrival, Philip Henslowe seemed to concentrate less on the playhouse and more on his other lucrative interests, which were **bullbaiting, bearbaiting,** and **brothels.** Alleyn retired from the stage in about 1597. However, he made a brief return shortly after 1600 and played the part of Genius for King James's procession into London in March 1604. He was wealthy enough to start a school and a hospital (now Dulwich College) southeast of London in 1613. He died in 1626.

In 1594, a group of actors, probably including many of those who had stayed with James Burbage at The Theatre, formed a new company. They gained the **patronage** of Lord Hunsdon, who was shortly to become **Lord Chamberlain.** The Queen's Men had disbanded in 1594, and a reorganization of the players seems to have taken place that summer. The main companies were the Admiral's Men and the Lord Chamberlain's Men. The Admiral's Men included Edward Alleyn and probably his brother John, George Attewell, James Tunstall, Thomas Downton, Richard Jones, the clown John Singer, Thomas Towne, Martin Slater, and Edward Juby. The Lord Chamberlain's Men included Thomas Pope, George Bryan, and the clown Will Kemp. These three had been with Leicester's Men in 1586 when they had performed at Elsinore in Denmark, the setting for Shakespeare's play *Hamlet.* Also in The Lord Chamberlain's Men were Augustine Phillips, John Heminges, Richard Cowley, John Sincler, William Sly, John Duke, Robert

Gough, and Richard Burbage. Also possibly included were Nicholas Tooley, Henry Condell, Alexander Cooke, and Christopher Beeston. William Shakespeare was almost certainly a member of this company, too. During June 1594, both companies were performing at The Rose. After that date, the **Chamberlain's** Men went back over the river to The Theatre, where they stayed until its closure in 1598.

Players who became **sharers** in their company were able to make a good deal of money. Not all players were sharers. Some were simply employees who were paid weekly, while others were **apprentices** of the more experienced men. Thomas Pope, for instance, was described as a "gentleman" when he died in 1604. This term implies that he had status and wealth. By 1619, Henry Condell was described as someone "of great living, wealth, and power." By 1625, he was living in a country house in Fulham. A clown named Thomas Sackville moved to Germany, where he invested in a silk business and died a rich man. Player-sharers who died poor, like Will Kemp, probably had only themselves to blame.

It is important to remember that there were no women in the playing companies in Shakespeare's time. All women's parts were played by boys or by men who specialized in female roles.

When the **Lord Chamberlain's** Men were formed, William Shakespeare was probably living in St. Helen's parish in the north of the city. This area is now east of Bishopsgate and bounded by Camomile Street and Crosby Square. It is known that he owned property there in 1596, because he was assessed for taxes. He failed to pay the full amount and was named as a defaulter a year later.

In October 1594, the Lord Chamberlain asked the city authorities to allow his company to use the Cross Keys Inn in Gracechurch Street, the southbound continuation of Bishopsgate, for winter performances and possibly for rehearsal purposes. The company played at court on December 26. Then, two days later, in the Hall of Gray's Inn, which was one of the centers of London's legal profession, they presented another play, *The Comedy of Errors* by William Shakespeare.

THE COMEDY OF ERRORS

For his first new work after the reopening of the playhouses, Shakespeare returned to the Latin plays he read at school. Plautus's *Menaechmi* was about a man searching for his twin brother. He is thrown into confusion when everyone he meets mistakes him for his twin brother. This play was performed by the boys of St. Paul's School in 1527. It was most likely a regular entertainment in schools and universities.

Shakespeare's *The Comedy of Errors* is a similar story to Plautus's *Menaechmi,* and it is as tightly constructed as any of the Latin plays after which it is modeled. Shakespeare doubles the potential for confusion with two sets of twins. He also makes the distinctively Shakespearean move of setting the play within a framework of death. Old Egeon, a merchant, is searching for his sons who were separated at birth. He has arrived at Ephesus from Syracuse despite a decree that any Syracusans found in the town will be executed. He is arrested and given a day to find someone to pay a ransom. Unknown to him, his son

Antipholus, of Syracuse, has also arrived with his servant Dromio, of Syracuse. The confusion begins as both the son and the servant are mistaken for their twin brothers, also named Antipholus and Dromio, who live in Ephesus.

The serious frame sets up dramatic possibilities. The unraveling of the confusion becomes a matter of life and death. It also enables Shakespeare to explore ideas about being a twin, which fascinated him. Shakespeare was the father of twins, Judith and Hamnet, born in 1585. Hamnet died at the age of 11 in August 1596. Shakespeare seems to have a deep understanding of what it means to be a twin and the pain of separation. Near the beginning of the play, Antipholus of Syracuse says,

> He that commends me to mine own content
> Commends me to the thing I cannot get.
> I to the world am like a drop of water
> That in the ocean seeks another drop. . .
>
> *The Comedy of Errors,* Act I Scene 2, lines 33–36

All the confusions are cleared up and mistakes put right. The brothers find one another, and Egeon finds his sons and long lost wife, who had become the abbess of a nunnery in Ephesus. The servant Dromio of Ephesus speaks at the end of the play.

> We came into the world like brother and brother,
> And now let's go hand in hand, not one before another.
>
> *The Comedy of Errors,* Act 5 Scene I, lines 429–430

Ephesus is a place of magic. It is famous in ancient times for witchcraft and sorcery. This, too, is an early indication of a theme that recurs throughout Shakespeare's later plays. In the real world of pain, death, and confusion, we need to step into another place where appearance and reality become confused. Only then can we discover the truth about ourselves.

A MIDSUMMER NIGHT'S DREAM

Over ten years later the tragic King Lear had to go into a stormy wilderness before he began to understand himself. But Shakespeare's own next place of mystery was a very English wood outside Athens.

A Midsummer Night's Dream was probably written in 1594 or 1595. There is no evidence to support the theory that it was written as part of a wedding celebration. Although one of its interlocking ideas is how marriage can bring differences together. *A Midsummer Night's Dream* has a range of sources and ideas, including transformations also found in Ovid's *Metamorphoses*. It brings together, too, many of the ideas Shakespeare has explored up to now: appearance and reality, separation and discovery, love and sex, hidden instincts and passions, the outward presentation of ourselves, and the natural and the supernatural.

Once more the framing technique is used. The play starts and finishes in Duke Theseus's palace in Athens. It opens as he prepares to marry Hippolyta, Queen of the Amazons. There is tension in the air. As the Duke reminds Hippolyta:

> . . . I wooed thee with my sword,
> And won thy love doing thee injuries.
> But I will wed thee in another key—
> With pomp, with triumph, and with revelling.
>
> *A Midsummer Night's Dream*, Act I Scene I, lines 16–19

Other tensions appear. Hermia is betrothed to Demetrius, but she is in love with Lysander. Demetrius loves Hermia, but he used to love Helena, who is still in love with him. Hermia and Lysander decide to run away through the forest to be married. Helena, hoping to get back into Demetrius's favor, tells him what the lovers are doing. Thus love becomes a source of confusion and a battleground.

Just as in *Love's Labour's Lost* and *The Two Gentlemen of Verona,* the romance is set against the antics of stock comic characters. In *A Midsummer Night's Dream,* the wood is filled not only with fleeing and pursuing lovers, but also with a group of workmen rehearsing a play that will be performed at the Duke's wedding. Peter Quince and his company are to play *The Most Lamentable Comedy and Most Cruel Death of Pyramus and Thisbe,* another story from Ovid. Again there is confusion. Is the workmen's play a **tragedy** or a comedy? A boy will play a girl—as they always did in Shakespeare's theater, except this time the confusion is told to the audience. A lion will roar "as gentle as any sucking dove."

Three layers of the play are quickly introduced. Then comes a fourth. The wood is home to the king and queen of the fairies, Oberon and Titania. They are in the middle of a bitter quarrel. Once more, tension is overcoming love, but now the effect is much greater. The quarrels of the fairies have affected the natural world.

> The spring, the summer,
> The chiding autumn, angry winter change
> Their wonted liveries, and the mazèd world

By their increase knows not which is which;
And this same progeny of evils comes
From our debate, from our dissension.
We are their parents and original.

A Midsummer Night's Dream, Act 2 Scene I, lines 111–117

The lovers, the workmen, and the fairies are all in the wood together. The tensions and confusions increase. So do the transformations. Oberon sends his servant, Puck, for a flower. The juice of the flower can be squeezed into someone's eye. This makes the person love the first thing he or she sees. With this flower, the fairies try to put the lovers' quarrel to rights, but they get it wrong. Lysander and Demetrius both transfer their love to Helena. Now the fairy king, Oberon, plays a cruel trick on the fairy queen, Titania. He squeezes the juice into her eyes. Then he transforms Bottom, the weaver, one of the workmen actors, into an ass. Oberon then makes sure Titania will see Bottom when she wakes. As soon as she sees him, she is full of desire and they go off to make love. Love and desire have disintegrated everywhere into fear and lust.

Eventually Oberon and Puck put things back as they should be. Lysander loves Hermia, Demetrius loves Helena, Titania and Oberon are reunited, and Bottom is changed back into a human being. There have been dreams, but none more amazing than Bottom's.

I have had a most rare vision. I have had a dream past the
wit of man to say what dream it was. Methought I was—
there is no man can tell what . . . It shall be called 'Bottom's
Dream' because it hath no bottom, and . . . I shall sing
it at her death.

A Midsummer Night's Dream, Act 4 Scene I, lines 202–206

Again, as the magic fades, Shakespearean ideas crowd together. The play has been full of complex and witty verse, but as the dream ends, we are left with simple, direct language. In the face of the deepest truth, words are not enough.

The earlier comic effect of mixing romance and **farce** is more integrated in this play. The multilayered world of fairies, kings, lovers, and clowns is shown as a single reality. Perhaps the whole play grows out of the marital and sexual anxieties of Theseus and Hippolyta. To win her, he must woo her. He must show her the layers of desire that true love requires.

A Midsummer Night's Dream is a disturbing and wonderful play of the imagination. There are transformations. People change. Their feelings change. Understanding changes. But like Adonis and the anemone at the end of "Venus and Adonis," one thing does not turn into another. Perhaps Shakespeare's great insight here is that the creative imagination works with resemblances. Things stay as they are— boys and flowers, weavers and asses, Amazon Queens and Fairy Queens. But they all gain new meaning from their likeness to each other.

Plays are no different. A player does not become his character of Puck or Bottom or Oberon. Rather, the player and character are there together in the same time and space. One of the functions of the performance of *Pyramus and Thisbe,* the small play within the play, is that it illuminates the themes in the larger play. Bottom is transformed again when he plays the lover Pyramus who loses Thisbe. But he is still Bottom the weaver, who has lost the Queen of the Fairies.

Even before this final story of love and separation, Duke Theseus and Hippolyta begin to understand.

Theseus: Such tricks hath strong imagination
That if it would but apprehend some joy
It comprehends some bringer of that joy;
Or in the night, imagining some fear,
How easy is a bush supposed a bear!

Hippolyta: But all the story of the night told over,
And all their minds transfigured so together,
More witnesseth than fancy's images,
And grows to something of great constancy;
But howsoever, strange and admirable.

A Midsummer Night's Dream, Act 5 Scene 1, lines 18–27

A Midsummer Night's Dream without bottom! In its final, most typical Shakespearean twist, the play remains open ended. The newlyweds go to bed. The fairies bless the house. Puck approaches with an apology. He says that if anyone is offended, they should see the play as "just a dream." But like any dream, it has no easy interpretation. It is not about this, nor is it about that.

Once more Shakespeare invites us in to the power of a play. Its meaning is uncertain and our own thoughts and feelings, hopes, and fears are part of it, too. In his last lines, Puck offers his hands to the audience. He invites the audience to join in the circle of imagination and understanding.

Give me your hands, if we be friends,
And Robin shall restore amends.

A Midsummer Night's Dream, Epilogue, lines 15–16

95

THE MERCHANT OF VENICE

During the later 1590s, Shakespeare wrote or contributed to at least 12 plays for his company. The tradition of love stories that began with *The Two Gentlemen of Verona* was developed in *Romeo and Juliet* and *Much Ado About Nothing*. His love stories became more complex with *The Merchant of Venice*.

By 1596 or 1597 when *The Merchant of Venice* was probably written, William Shakespeare was an experienced man of the theater. He was more and more able to put together plays with many layers of plot and meaning. On the surface, *The Merchant of Venice* seems to be a simple story. It is about a wicked Jew who is trying to trick and kill Christians, but he is being outsmarted. The play is full of insight into human nature. It deals with serious matters, though it can raise smiles as well. Darkness and pain are never far away. *The Merchant of Venice* has been criticized for being anti-Semitic, that is prejudiced against Jews, in order to have a comic effect. But the more closely the play is examined, the more interpretations it has.

First of all, it is about a merchant. In 1598, it was referred to as *"The Merchant of Venice* or otherwise called *The Jew of Venice."* Already in the title there is uncertainty. Is the central character Antonio, the Christian merchant, or is it the Jew named Shylock? They are both concerned with trade. The play is about love and friendship, but these are linked with making deals and taking chances. They are also linked with honesty and trust. In his play *The Taming of the Shrew,* Shakespeare showed that marriage proposals can be conducted like trade deals. In a world where marriages were often basically business deals, his audience would understand what was going on.

The play is about a merchant and a moneylender. Antonio and Shylock have something the other one wants. The Christian wants the Jew's money in order to finance his business arrangements. Shylock, the Jew, wants the respect and social standing that as a Jew he cannot have. Shakespeare himself grew up in the world of trade and never wholly left it behind. His father was a merchant and a moneylender. Almost certainly William was, too. His father was nearly imprisoned for debt. The world of this play was one Shakespeare knew well.

A second interpretation of *The Merchant of Venice* is about justice. Antonio has borrowed money to finance his friend Bassanio's attempt to marry Portia. Portia is a rich heiress. When Antonio is unable to repay the debt, Shylock takes him to a court of law. The battle between Shylock and the lawyer Balthasar, who is really Portia in disguise, is a debate between those who stand by "the letter of the law" and those who are prepared to show mercy. It is too simple to say that this is a battle between Jewish and Christian ideas. Shakespeare shows how both sides lock themselves into a merciless struggle for revenge.

This is also a debate about trade. The 1500s saw an important shift in English law. Medieval law was a system in which compromise was rarely possible. Justice sided with the one who had the best case. But in the 1500s new practices developed that were more suited to trade. The harsh effects of a law could be reduced through agreement and compromise. Shylock refuses to compromise, but it is clear that without this position, he is without power. He can rely only on the strict letter of justice. When that is taken away by Balthasar, Shylock is a broken man.

A third interpretation of *The Merchant of Venice* looks at what it means to be an outsider. It explores the possibility of toleration. The play appears to be anti-Semitic because so many of its characters hate Jews. There is no reason to believe that Shakespeare agreed with them. The Christians of Venice go for Shylock like a pack of wolves. But each time he appears—in six of the play's twenty scenes—he is seen as a complex man. He is vulnerable and defiant, witty yet calculating. He is a man acting out what his situation demands. With a glimpse of the real Shylock, the cost of being an outsider is revealed. If he turns the other cheek, he will not survive.

> I am a Jew. If you tickle us do we not laugh? If you poison us do we not die? And if you wrong us shall we not revenge?. . . The villainy you teach me I will execute, and it shall go hard but I will better the instruction.
>
> *The Merchant of Venice*, Act 3 Scene 1, lines 54–67

THE HISTORY PLAYS

The other strand of playwriting that Shakespeare developed in the later 1590s was the history play. He had made a name for himself some years earlier with his great tetralogy, or set of four plays. The tetralogy explored the upheaval of the Wars of the Roses. It ended with the victory of Queen Elizabeth I's grandfather, King Henry VII, over King Richard III. Those plays began with the death of King Henry V.

Now Shakespeare explored how kings prepare for kingship and exercise their kingship when they have it.

For the Middle Ages, the right to rule involved the power to rule. The king should be the strongest of the nobles. A weak king was likely to be overthrown. But there was also the problem of succession. A kingship should pass from father to son. As Shakespeare had shown in his plays about I Ienry VI, Edward IV, and Richard III, political, economic, and moral stability depended on closing the gap between might and right. It depended on making sure that the rightful ruler could overcome opposition.

In *King John,* probably written in 1595 or 1596, Shakespeare focuses on the struggle between King John and another claimant to the throne, Philip Falconbridge. Falconbridge was the illegitimate son of Richard I. He may be the best man to be king, but he is barred from the throne by John because his father was not married to his mother. However, John's own weak right to be king unleashes disorder in the land.

King John introduces a second idea that is crucial to the history plays of *Richard II, Henry IV Parts 1 and 2,* and *Henry V*. These plays deal with power and legitimacy. Shakespeare connects power and legitimacy with a single question, "Who is my father?" This is a political question: "Who gives me the right to be what I am?" It is a moral question: "Whom do I want to be like?" It is also a practical question: "How shall I present myself?"

Richard II was probably written in 1595. It shows a king at war within himself. He has the right to be king, but his unlawful actions of banishing those who oppose him and confiscating their possessions, leads to a rebellion. He is deposed and eventually murdered by Henry Bolingbroke, who is now Duke of Lancaster. Bolingbroke has a weaker right to rule, but he has the might to control the kingdom. Victory in battle, however, makes Bolingbroke a legitimate heir.

> **York:** Great Duke of Lancaster, I come to thee
> From plume-plucked Richard, who with willing soul
> Adopts thee heir, and his high sceptre yields
> To the possession of thy royal hand.
> Ascend his throne, decending now from him,
> And long live Henry, of that name the fourth!
>
> *Richard II,* Act 4 Scene 1, lines 98–103

Bolingbroke may now be legitimate, but he is a troubled man. His last words in the play are full of guilt for what he has done.

> Lords, I protest my soul is full of woe
> That blood should sprinkle me to make me grow. . .
> I'll make a voyage to the Holy Land
> To wash this blood off from my guilty hand.'
>
> *Richard II,* Act 5 Scene 6, lines 45–50

Richard II takes place entirely in the world of court politics. With the two plays of *Henry IV,* Shakespeare takes us on a journey through England, palaces, taverns, country gardens, and battlefields. He also introduces one of his most famous characters, the rollickingly overweight and immortally immoral Sir John Falstaff. Falstaff was so popular that he was reborn in 1597 in the comedy *The Merry Wives of Windsor.* It was probably written for the celebrations following **Lord Chamberlain** Hunsdon's installation as a **Knight of the Garter** at Windsor. In the earliest performances of *Henry IV*, Falstaff was called Sir John Oldcastle, who was a real historical figure. The name was changed under pressure from Oldcastle's descendants, the Cobham family. One of the Cobhams was Lord Chamberlain between August 1596 and March 1597. This probably dates the first performance of *Henry IV Part 1* to the first half of 1596.

The change from the seriousness of *Richard II* to the wide range of the *Henry* plays is not simply to make them more entertaining. Henry IV's son, Prince Hal, will legitimately be king because his father is. He has to make crucial decisions about what sort of king he will be. This will also decide what sort of man he will be. These choices are dramatized in the triangular relationship between Henry, Hal, and Falstaff.

Hal moves between two worlds. One is headed by the guilt-ridden Henry, who is weighed down by the affairs of state and from whom Hal can learn about responsibility and duty. The other world is the alternative court of Falstaff and his disreputable pals at the Boar's Head Tavern. Falstaff appears at times to be a lovable rogue. Young Prince Hal enjoys his company. But it gradually becomes clear that the older man is a criminal, a man without honor, and a man with no respect for the law or for other people.

As Hal experiences England in all its variety, so this young prince is brought to the great moment of choice. Will he be like Henry or like Falstaff? Who will be his true father?

The choice is made more urgent by another rebellion. Powerful families from the North and from Wales want to overthrow Henry. Young Harry Percy, also known as Hotspur, is the most charismatic of the rebels. He prompts another triangular relationship. Henry cannot help but see Hotspur as the son he would have preferred. Hal is all too aware of how his father feels. How a child lives up to a parent's expectations is also an issue in the plays.

All these matters are focused on one great scene toward the end of *Henry IV Part 2*. The king, close to death, prepares to pass the crown on to his son. With dramatic effect, the crown, a sign of the anxieties that press upon any king, passes between king and prince. First Hal removes it without permission from the sleeping king. When Henry wakes, he is furious that the crown has been taken. He believes that Hal's links with Falstaff will prevent Hal from ruling wisely.

> . . . the fifth Harry from curbed licence plucks
> The muzzle of restraint, and the wild dog
> Shall flesh his tooth on every innocent.
>
> *Henry IV Part 2*, Act 4 Scene 3, lines 259–261

But Hal has already recognized which way he must turn. He will change and be Henry's son. He will pick up the responsibilities of the kingdom. Shakespeare shows Hal's choice in its starkest terms in the final scene. Hal has been crowned Henry V. Falstaff comes to beg favors for himself and his friends, but the new king crushes him.

> I know thee not, old man. Fall to thy prayers . . .
> Presume not that I am the thing I was,
> For God doth know, so shall the world perceive,
> That I have turned away my former self.
>
> *Henry IV Part 2*, Act 5 Scene 5, lines 47, 56–58

Kings are known by how they show themselves to the world. Kings and queens are actors, always in role, always presenting themselves as in a play. In the history plays, Shakespeare reveals a deep understanding of the essence of politics, which is to keep power by showing power. Shakespeare shows, too, the inner costs of power and kingship. Rulers may be racked by guilt or uncertainty, but failing to display their right to rule opens up a gap that others will rush in to fill.

Henry V was written in 1599. It is probably the last play Shakespeare wrote for the **Lord Chamberlain's Men** before they left The Theatre. Their new home would be across the river at The Globe. *Henry V* is often seen as a triumphant celebration of English greatness, a propaganda piece. But Shakespeare is showing rebellion, uncertainty, error, arrogance, and the horrors of war. Henry V is the man who was Prince Hal, aware of his wild youth. He was aware, too, of his father's pain and guilt.

Henry is good at presenting himself to the public as a king. He magnificently displays his power. But he has a private side, too, like his father. On the night before the battle of Agincourt, he disguises himself and goes around the camp listening to his soldiers. They are afraid. Joining a small group he tries to encourage them by saying that the coming battle will be for a just cause, so they need not fear death. One of the soldiers, Michael Williams, answers him.

> But if the cause be not good, the King himself hath a
> heavy reckoning to make, when all those legs and arms
> and heads chopped off in a battle shall join together at

the latter day. . . I am afeard there are few die well that
die in battle. . . Now if these men do not die well, it will be
a black matter for the King that led them to it. . .

Henry V, Act 2 Scene 1, lines 133–144

Later, when Henry is alone, he admits to himself what
it really means to be a ruler. In words that recall his
father's agony ("Uneasy lies the head that wears a
crown," *Henry IV Part 2,* act 3 scene 1, line 31),
Henry V acknowledges that

'Tis not the balm the sceptre and the ball,
The sword, the mace the crown imperial. . .
The throne he sits on, nor the tide of pomp
That beats upon the high shore of this world—
No, not all these, laid in bed majestical,
Can sleep so soundly as the wretched slave. . .

Henry V, Act 4 Scene 1, lines 257–265

8
THE GLOBE

By the end of 1598, William Shakespeare was a highly successful player and playwright with the **Lord Chamberlain's** Men. They had become one of the two most important companies in London. Their only serious opposition at this time were the Admiral's Men. The Admiral's Men were still based at Philip Henslowe's playhouse, The Rose, on the south bank of the Thames River.

Shakespeare's success was shown in his increasing wealth and status. This must have contributed to an improvement in the Shakespeare family fortunes. In the late 1560s, John Shakespeare applied for a coat-of-arms, a public sign of status. Because his business was not going well, he was unable to continue the application. But in October 1596, the coat-of-arms was granted. John Shakespeare was described as a man worth about $3,000. This was a small fortune at a time when a laborer earned about 30 cents a week.

The motto *Non Sanz Droict*, old French meaning "Not Without Right," may have been added to the Shakespeare coat-of-arms. There is no evidence that the family used the motto. Although Shakespeare's colleague, Ben Jonson, in his 1599 play *Every Man Out of His Humour,* has a character who buys his coat-of-arms with the motto "Not Without Mustard." This may be a parody of Shakespeare's motto.

The granting of a coat-of-arms to the family was probably helped by Shakespeare's wealth. His wealth supported his father's financial improvement and helped to pay for the processing of the application.

The next year, Shakespeare reinforced his and the family's status by buying the second largest house in Stratford. It was called New Place. The house and garden were located at the corner of Chapel Street and Chapel Lane, near the Guild Chapel. It is estimated that he paid William Underhill about $73 for the property. Five years later, Shakespeare bought a cottage in Chapel Lane and a lot of land just outside the town. He also made other investments in Stratford during the following years. These deals would have made him an important man in Stratford.

There is one small but satisfying coincidence hidden in these deals. Before the **bailiff** and **aldermen** of Stratford were given responsibility for the repair of the bridge over the river in the 1550s, the cost of its upkeep was paid for with money raised from the annual play of St. George and the Dragon. In 1598, Shakespeare provided leftover stone from New Place for the repair of the bridge. Once again, the work on Stratford's bridge was funded by plays.

In London, times were changing for the **Lord Chamberlain's** Men. The lease on The Theatre was due to run out, and the company was in disagreement with the owner of the land, Giles Allen. Their situation was made more difficult when playing companies were no longer favored by the authorities. This was because a play called *The Isle of Dogs* appeared to be making fun of the royal court.

The actors responsible for the play *The Isle of Dogs* were a new group called Pembroke's Men. They were performing at The Swan, which was in the **Liberty** of the Manor of Paris Gardens on the south bank of the river. The Swan was built in 1595 by Francis Langley, a city financier. It was located very near The Rose in an attempt to steal The Rose's audience. Pembroke's Men was probably the Swan's resident company.

The offense caused by *The Isle of Dogs* had an immediate but short term effect on the other companies. They were soon back in action. However, the dispute with Giles Allen rumbled on. The Lord Chamberlain's Men moved out of The Theatre and played for a short time at The Curtain. By the end of 1598, it was clear that there would be no agreement with Allen. He even threatened to demolish the playhouse. But then it appears that the Lord Chamberlain's Men found a legal loophole that would allow them to remove the building from the site.

On December 28, 1598, Richard Burbage, his brother Cuthbert, their mother, a carpenter, a builder, and about 12 laborers set to work dismantling The Theatre on its site to the north of the city. They took it, piece by piece, through the streets and over the river to a site not far from The Rose and The Swan. Then they began to rebuild it. The new playhouse was finished before May 1599.

Henslowe's account books show that The Theatre was already a dangerous rival. With fewer profits at The Rose, Henslowe and Edward Alleyn decided to move north of the river. Their new theater, called The Fortune, was in the Liberty of Finsbury between the present Whitecross Street and Golden Lane. There still is a Fortune Street there today. The Fortune was constructed in 1600 and was built by Peter Streete. Streete had helped the Burbages dismantle The Theatre

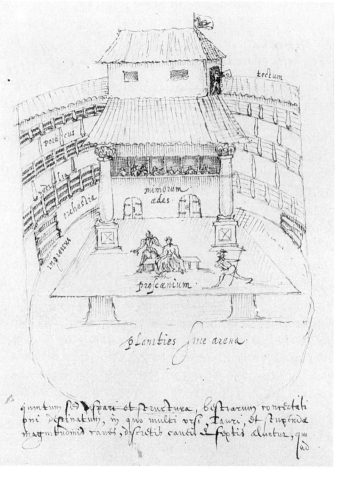

This is a copy of a drawing by Johannes de Witt done in 1596 of The Swan theater. The copy was done by Arnout Van Buchell.

and build their new playhouse. The star actor, Edward Alleyn, even made a brief return to the stage, perhaps to revive the Admiral's Men in their new playhouse.

The new playhouse of the **Lord Chamberlain's** Men was called The Globe. The flag that flew above the stage bore the Latin motto, *Totus Mundus Agit Histrionem.* This translates to "All the world's a stage." The play of *Henry V* had a character known as **Chorus,** who sets the scene for the action and comments on it. Part of Chorus's function is to point to the similarities and differences between history and the action of the play.

> . . . pardon, gentles all,
> The flat unraisèd spirits that hath dared
> On this unworthy scaffold to bring forth
> So great an object. Can this cock-pit hold
> The vasty fields of France? Or may we cram
> Within this wooden O the very casques
> That did affright the air at Agincourt?
>
> *Henry V,* Act I Scene I, lines 8–14

The questions of Chorus invite the answer, "Yes, we can," as long as imagination is present.

> And let us . . . on your imaginary forces work . . .
> Think, when we talk of horses, that you see them . . .

As Duke Theseus said of the players toward the end of *A Midsummer Night's Dream,*

> The best in this kind are but shadows, and the worst are no worse if imagination amend them.

Hippolyta ironically responds.

> It must be your imagination, then, and not theirs.
>
> *A Midsummer Night's Dream*, Act 5 Scene 1, lines 210-212

Players and the audience shared in making a playhouse a place of the imagination.

GOING TO THE GLOBE

> After dinner on the 21st September, at about two o'clock, I went with my companions over the water, and in the strewn roof-house saw the **tragedy** of the first Emperor Julius with at least fifteen characters very well acted. At the end of the comedy they danced according to their custom, with extreme elegance. Two in men's clothes and two in women's gave this performance, in wonderful combination with each other.

This account by Thomas Platter, a Swiss visitor to London, is about an early performance of *Julius Caesar* at The Globe. Some scholars think this was the first play at the new playhouse. But since The Globe was completed, or nearly completed, by May 1599, this seems unlikely. Others suggest that *Henry V,* a spectacular play, or *As You Like It,* with its famous speech that begins "All the world's a stage," are possibly the first plays.

It is not known how the **Lord Chamberlain's** Men chose to open their new playhouse. But Platter's account and other evidence, such as the plays themselves, give valuable information about how The Globe was built, financed, and used.

The Globe was built using the timbers of The Theatre. It probably was similar to the older theater's basic construction. The Globe was probably a 20-sided polygon. It would look almost circular. It was between 90 and 100 feet (27 and 30 meters) in diameter and had a thatched roof. It is not known how The Globe looked inside, but it would have had a raised stage. The actual size of the stage is unknown. Other playhouses of the time had stages that were about 44 feet (13 meters) wide by 25 feet (8 meters) deep.

The area in front of the stage was for standing customers. The two galleries on three sides had benches or seats for wealthier playgoers. Behind the stage was the **tiring house** for costume changes, props, and scenery. It was also a general gathering place for the company.

The Globe, like the other playhouses, was a very flexible space. The tiring house contained machinery that allowed special effects or actors to be "flown" in by suspending them on ropes. The special effects or the actors could be lowered to the stage or suspended in the air. The stage had trapdoors for quick exits and entrances. There were balconies for lovers, battlements for soldiers, and alcoves that could be curtained off. Its open stage could be a room or the sea, a forest or a city street. Above all, it was an intimate, enclosed space that focused attention on the stage and allowed imagination to take flight.

Old James Burbage died in 1597. The dealings with Giles Allen about the lease on The Theatre were carried out by his sons Cuthbert and Richard. They probably negotiated the agreement to lease the land on the Bankside for the new playhouse. But when the lease was signed, seven men were named as **sharers** in The Globe.

This is a self-portrait by Richard Burbage (1567–1619). He was the chief actor of the King's Men and the first actor to perform the roles of Hamlet and King Lear.

One half-share was split between Cuthbert and Richard Burbage. The other half share was divided between five of the **Lord Chamberlain's** Men: Thomas Pope, Augustine Phillips, John Heminges, the clown Will Kemp, and William Shakespeare.

To be a **sharer** in the profits from a playhouse was another step towards becoming wealthy. The group changed over the years, and the shares changed hands. For instance, Thomas Pope died in 1604. Will Kemp left the company before the end of 1599 to strike out on his own.

Kemp was a clown famous for his jigs. He probably created the roles of Bottom in *A Midsummer Night's Dream* and Costard in *Love's Labour's Lost*. It is likely that he was a court jester for the Earl of Leicester. He was more like a stand-up comic than a theater company man. After leaving the Lord Chamberlain's Men, he undertook a marathon solo performance from London to Norwich and wrote a book about it. He died in poverty and probably from the **plague** in 1603.

There is no obvious clown's role for Kemp in *Julius Caesar*. It is possible that he had already stopped working at The Globe by September 1599. Platter remarks that the jig was performed by "two men and two women." Most likely the women were men dressed as women. This might suggest that Kemp was not one of them, but the fact that there was a jig may mean he was there.

The jig traditionally ended the plays. It was like a bawdy curtain call. The jig was popular with Elizabethan playgoers, and Kemp was one of their favorites. But tastes changed. The jigs continued at lower-class theaters, such as The Curtain or The Fortune, but the jigs were no longer part of the serious playhouses.

The Globe set out to establish itself as a playhouse for a better class of audience. From 1599, Shakespeare's plays began to adopt a different tone. This may have been to satisfy a different playgoing audience.

If "all the world's a stage," then people may have wanted to see on stage a world that is in order. No matter what confusions reign, everything on stage turns out well. Many of Shakespeare's plays can be read in a way that all is well that ends well. But when performed, his plays become ambiguous. By the end no one is wholly good or completely bad. No one is completely happy, and nothing is absolutely certain.

JULIUS CAESAR

The opening of *Julius Caesar* is a great shock. A crowd tumbles onto the stage in a carnival mood. They are sent away. But all through the play, the energy of the crowd and danger of the mob are never far away.

In the late 1590s, economic unrest and rebellion were in the air. By 1599, the government and the London authorities were very suspicious of large gatherings. This is one of the reasons for the ban on players' performances. In his plays, Shakespeare showed the wealthy citizens what they were afraid of. After Caesar is killed, the same carnival crowd turns into a lynch mob. The mob tears Cinna, the poet, to pieces.

Shakespeare's use of the crowd in *Julius Caesar* is complex. The play is set in ancient Rome. It is set at a time when its citizens were trying to find ways of controlling powerful individuals and families. A republic had been established to share power between different sections of the community. Some feared that Julius Caesar's victorious return from war might get him proclaimed as emperor. This would return Rome to the bad old days of tyranny and cruelty. Will Caesar's ambition mean the end of the Roman republic? Two Romans, Cassius and Brutus, are afraid that it will. They arrange a secret meeting with others of the same view. Together they decide that Caesar must die so that the republic will survive.

Here is another crowd in the middle of Rome. The conspirators may be noblemen and senators, but how different are they from the rabble who will kill Cinna? As the conspirators debate between themselves, there is both language and silence. Language persuades and may drive us into action. After the words, there is only the silence of the dead Caesar and the dead Cinna.

There are differences between Cassius and Brutus. Brutus is an idealist. He is committed to the Roman ideal of republicanism. He is opposed to Caesar because Caesar threatens that ideal. As Cassius and Brutus debate, it becomes clear that Cassius's persuasive tongue hides his less pure motives. There is some of Caesar's pride and ambition in him, too.

After the conspirators have killed Caesar, they realize that they need to persuade the people in the crowd that they have acted in the crowd's best interests.

Brutus speaks to them and appears to win them over.

> Romans, countrymen, and lovers, hear me for my
> cause, and be silent that you may hear. . .
> Who is here so rude that would not be a Roman?. . .
> Who is here so vile that will not love his country?
>
> *Julius Caesar,* Act 3 Scene 2, lines 13, 30, 32

Brutus's speech is a model of persuasive political **oratory**. Shakespeare writes the speech in prose to make it more direct. After he has finished, Caesar's close friend Mark Antony approaches the conspirators. Mark Antony asks to address the crowd. He promises to reinforce Brutus's arguments. Cassius is reluctant, but Brutus agrees.

Mark Antony's famous speech, in verse with many **rhetorical** flourishes, plays on ideas of ambition and honor. It appears to applaud the conspirators, but it ends with an appeal to the greedy mob, prompting them to howl for the blood of Brutus and Cassius.

Under the cover of reasonable argument, Mark Antony whips up emotion.

> [Brutus] Hath told you Caesar was ambitious
> . . . And Brutus is an honourable man

He continues by saying,

> I fear I wrong the honourable men
> Whose daggers have stabbed Caesar. . .

and he concludes with irony.

> I am no orator as Brutus is,
> But were I Brutus,
> And Brutus Antony, there were an Antony
> Would ruffle up your spirits, and put a tongue

In every wound of Caesar that should move
The stones of Rome to rise and mutiny.

Julius Caesar, Act 3 Scene 2, lines 78–79, 88, 152–153, 212, 221–225

Antony's speech is a superb example of rhetoric. It is highly patterned, complex language. It seems to say one thing, while all the time implying something else. It appeals to the emotions rather than reason. In its typically Shakespearean masterstroke, it relies on silence to make its most telling point—when Mark Antony uncovers the bloody body of Caesar. The boy from Stratford **grammar school** learned his lessons about the arts of persuasion well.

Within the rhetoric of drama, Antony's speech is a highly dramatic act. It addresses the crowds and changes their allegiance. At the same time, it addresses the playgoing audience, drawing it into the crowd in ancient Rome.

The stage of The Globe was suited to such a double action. The actor playing Antony could come close to the playgoers standing in front of the stage. They stood like a crowd. They were not seated like an audience. Mark Antony could address them directly. This is the power that made city authorities fear the playhouses. At the end, while staying true to the story, Shakespeare leaves his audience, with the wealthier ones sitting safely in the galleries, no comfort. The careful idealist Brutus dies. The rabble-rousing Antony takes power.

As You Like It

Another play that could also be the first play performed at The Globe takes place in a mysterious wood. This wood is both in the Ardennes in France and the very English Forest of Arden. Arden is the area to the north and west of Stratford. It is a wintry landscape peopled with outlaws. *As You Like It* is one of Shakespeare's plays that people have tried to make romantic and pretty. In fact, it is a tough exploration of love. It contrasts town and country. It looks at power misused and resisted.

The world shown in *As You Like It* is close to economic, social, and moral collapse. There is poverty and famine. Brothers are stealing the inheritances of brothers. The play seems to mirror a time in the late 1590s when a series of disastrous harvests caused social tension. The Forest of Arden was a violent place in the 1590s. It was full of poverty, feuding, outlaws, and assaults. This was caused by the changing economy in the countryside. *As You Like It* is full of the usual things found in plays and poems. It even has shepherds and shepherdesses dancing under blue skies.

But the reality is quite different and is summed up in the song of Amiens, a lord who has become an outlaw.

> Blow, blow thou winter wind,
> Thou art not so unkind
>   As man's ingratitude.
> Thy tooth is not so keen,
> Because thou art not seen,
>   Although thy breath be rude.
> Hey-ho, sing hey-ho, unto the green holly.
> Most friendship is feigning, most loving, mere folly.
>   Then hey-ho, the holly;
>   This life is most jolly.

As You Like It, Act 2 Scene 7, lines 175–184

In *As You Like It,* Shakespeare paints a picture of different types of love and friendship. At the beginning of the play, we see two destructive relationships between brothers. Duke Frederick has usurped the land of his brother, Duke Senior, and banished him into the forest. Orlando, the youngest son of Duke Frederick's old enemy, Sir Rowland de Bois, is being ill-treated by his older brother Oliver, and he escapes into the forest.

Contrasted with this are faithful friendships. There is a friendship between Orlando and his old servant Adam. There is another friendship between Rosalind, Duke Senior's daughter, and Celia, the daughter of Duke Frederick.

Rosalind and Orlando fall in love. Then Rosalind, disguised as a boy so that she'll be safe in the dangerous forest, educates Orlando in the practicalities of love, friendship, and marriage.

Other pairs of lovers meet in the forest. There is the romantic affair of Silvius and Phoebe. Another pair is the uncomplicated relationship between Touchstone, an urban character out of place in the forest, and the countrygirl, Audrey. Duke Senior and Orlando eventually return to their rightful places in society. The lovers prepare for marriage under the watchful eye of Hymen, god of marriage.

However, the play does not quite end there. One of the men banished to the forest with Duke Senior is Jaques. Jaques' serious temperament regularly reminds the others that the world is full of pain and that joys are short-lived. He is the character who speaks of all the world being a stage.

> And all the men and women merely players.
> They have their exits and their entrances. . .
>
> *As You Like It*, Act 2 Scene 7, lines 140–141

After Hymen has blessed the marriages, Jaques offers a serious assessment of what awaits the pairs of lovers. Then he goes to live as a hermit in the forest.

> So, to your pleasures;
> I am for other than for dancing measures.
>
> *As You Like It*, Act 5 Scene 4, lines 190–191

THE MASTER OF THE REVELS

The **Lord Chamberlain's** Men had a particularly close relationship with the officials whose job was to provide entertainments for the queen and her court. These officials were also the ones that censored every play before it could be performed. Their job was to make sure each play contained nothing that would offend the queen or her friends and allies.

The Lord Chamberlain was the chief officer of the court, responsible for everyone who might come in contact with the queen. This included those who served at meals and assisted in her private quarters. It also included those who looked after her clothes, jewels, palaces, and weapons collection.

The Lord Chamberlain also supervised the people who tended to the queen's spiritual well-being—the clergy and choir of the Chapel Royal—as well as her musicians, physicians, library staff, gardeners, and the masters of her hunting dogs. The Lord Chamberlain arranged the royal entertainments, too. Much of this work for the entertainment was given to officials known as the Revels Office. But the Lord Chamberlain undoubtedly took an active interest, especially if the queen was likely to be present at an event.

During Queen Elizabeth's reign, Shakespeare's company worked for three Lord Chamberlains. They worked for Henry Carey, 1st Lord Hunsdon. He held the office between 1585 and 1596, He created the Lord Chamberlain's Men in 1594. Next, the company worked for William Brooke, Lord Cobham, from 1596 to 1598. Their final Lord Chamberlain was Henry Carey's son, George, 2nd Lord Hunsdon. He was Chamberlain from 1598 until the queen's death in 1603. It was George Carey's brother, Richard, who rode from London to Edinburgh to tell James the news that he was King of England.

The Revels Office had a **Master of the Revels**, one or two clerks, and a Yeoman. At first the, Yeoman was a tailor. His job was to maintain the wardrobe of clothes. Later, the Yeoman helped to prepare for court performances. In 1599 the Yeoman was Edward Kirkham. The Revels Office organized and paid for the court performances of playing companies. It also maintained a collection of costumes, props, and scenery. In general, it watched over the London theater scene. They licensed plays, companies, and playhouses. In theory, nothing happened on the stage of a London playhouse that had not been approved first by the Master of the Revels.

The first Master with whom Shakespeare worked was Sir Edmund Tilney. He was responsible for gathering the Queen's Men in 1583. He remained in office until 1607, when he was succeeded by his nephew Sir George Buc.

Licensing involved a fee, which, in true Elizabethan and **Jacobean** fashion, helped increase the wealth of the official who issued the license. Tilney gradually raised his fees to 7 shillings, or about 56 cents, for a new play. That equaled about 84 one-penny standing places in a playhouse. Tilney also required the companies to pay 5 shillings, or about 40 cents, for each week that their playhouse was open. Sir George Buc's fees went up to £1, about $1.60, for issuing a license to perform a play. He charged another £1 for permission to print a play.

Playing companies called to perform before the queen may have earned as much as £10, about $16, for a show. This was probably as much as they could make with one full house in an outdoor theater. But being at court brought prestige. Being at court brought the added luxury of being warm and dry.

MASQUES

As well as authorizing companies to perform, the Revels Office also managed the costly productions known as **masques**. They were very popular during the reign of James I. A masque was a lavish entertainment of music, dance, and words. It involved elaborate staging and was very expensive to produce. Ladies and gentlemen of the court often took part. This was the only theatrical performances where women could be on stage. Professional players and musicians took part as well.

The architect and designer Inigo Jones was a famous creator of the visual elements of masques. Many of which were written by Shakespeare's fellow-playwright, Ben Jonson. There is no record of any masques being written by Shakespeare. Although it is quite likely that he participated in the masques as a member of the **Lord Chamberlain's** Men and the King's Men.

The stagecraft and formal structure of masques influenced Shakespeare. The masques were often based on themes from ancient Greek and Roman mythology. The stories were altered in order to heap praise on King James. Many of Shakespeare's plays after 1605 include scenes of formal dancing or song. They sometimes involve mythical characters, who added a deeper layer to the action.

CENSORSHIP

As well as organizing events at court and raising money by issuing licenses, the Revels Office had an important censorship function. The opportunity for players to give offense or to make libelous, blasphemous, or treasonable statements on stage was always an anxiety for **Tudor** governments. It has remained so for governments ever since. Censorship in the British theater only ended in 1968.

Government censorship of plays and players probably began as a way of preventing the **Corpus Christi** plays from becoming a focus for **Catholic** sympathizers. Censorship developed in two ways. First, it ensured that only appropriate plays would be presented at court. Sir Edmund Tilney's original job seems to have been to ensure that the queen got acceptable entertainment as cheaply as possible. Second, it reinforced state control over information to minimize the risk of dissent and rebellion.

Nevertheless, by the 1590s, there was a clear structure. Playing companies were required to submit new work to the **Master of the Revels.** He would charge a fee to read it. He would make notes on it and send it back with instructions for changes. He would not issue a license to perform it unless the changes were made.

Sometime in the early 1590s, a group of playwrights collaborated on a play about Sir Thomas More. More was the Lord Chancellor in the government of Henry VIII. More opposed the king's divorce from Catherine of Aragon. He was imprisoned and then eventually executed. The play was submitted to Tilney who clearly thought that it was politically unacceptable. He asked for many changes to be made. It is unclear what happened next, but it seems most likely that the play was put away for a few years. It was brought out again after the queen died in 1603.

Tilney's notes provide a fascinating insight into the boundaries that players must not cross.

> Leave out the insurrection wholy & the Cause ther off & begin with Sr Tho: Moore at the mayors sessions with a reportt afterwardes off his good service don being Shrive [Sheriff] of London upon a mutiny Agaynst the Lumbardes only by A shortt reporte & nott otherwise at your own perilles.
>
> E. Tilney

In other words, the players had to cut the scenes that showed riots against foreigners. There were similar riots in London in the 1590s. The scenes might have inflamed an already dangerous situation. Later in the play, the players were told to cut the scene in which More refuses to obey the king. But Tilney did not ban the play altogether, although it showed a **Catholic** martyr. He gave suggestions for changing it to make it acceptable. Plays could take risks, but only to a point.

The play of *Sir Thomas More* includes two scenes that may have been written by Shakespeare. It still exists in manuscript form. It is possible that one section is in his own handwriting. It is the scene with the riots against foreigners. If it is by Shakespeare, then it is not known whether he wrote it before it was submitted to Tilney, or if it was written after the death of Queen Elizabeth, ignoring Tilney's demands.

By the time *Julius Caesar* and *As You Like It* were being performed at The Globe, Shakespeare was nearly 36 years old. He was an experienced actor and playwright. He was also a successful and wealthy businessman. He and his fellow players had learned their trade in a number of playing companies from the 1580s onwards. Now, as the **Lord Chamberlain's** Men, they were one of the two most successful companies in London. They had regular performances at the royal court, and they toured the country.

With success came wealth and the opportunity for increased professionalism. The players were highly skilled. The system of **apprenticeships** ensured that young actors were well-trained. Staging techniques became increasingly better. The playwrights of the time responded to these new possibilities by creating increasingly complex situations.

The new styles of plays were also demanding new responses from actors. They were learning to balance royal approval and censorship. They were learning how to be popular with both a broad audience and the refined atmosphere of the court.

9
THE KING'S MEN

In May 1603, the **Lord Chamberlain's** Men received a royal warrant and became the King's Men. Queen Elizabeth's Lord Chamberlain, George Carey, had ceremonially broken his white stick of office on her death. He was not reappointed. Instead, he was replaced by Thomas Howard, who was soon made Earl of Suffolk. Under Howard and Sir George Buc, **Master of the Revels**, the new company developed a relationship with the court.

King James was a great believer in displaying the magnificence of his court. He expected the plays chosen for his entertainment to be spectacular. He also loved intellectual arguments and wanted his plays to be interesting explorations of ideas. The King's Men responded to this new atmosphere.

For Shakespeare, the new atmosphere was colored by a deeper cynicism. In the last years of Queen Elizabeth's reign, a sense of decay had begun to creep into his work. The framework of death and disorder, in which he had set many of his comedies and love stories, also began to frame his plots of love and friendship. The political awareness of his history plays became even more complex. The gap between words and actions, and between public statements and private intentions, became even greater.

Shakespeare's own business affairs improved during these years. As a **sharer** in the **Chamberlain's** Men and King's Men, he had a cut of the profits from the plays and from ticket sales at The Globe. In addition he kept in touch with Stratford. He was involved in a number of business deals at this time.

The attack on Shakespeare in *Greene's Groatsworth of Wit* in 1592 had accused him, among other things, of being a moneylender and a hoarder. The accusations may be true.

During 1598, two fellow citizens of Stratford, Abraham Sturley and Richard Quiney, were in London on Stratford business. They were in debt. Richard received advice from his father, Adrian Quiney, who was in Stratford. The father suggested that his son should "bargain with Mr. Sha." Mr. Sha would be William Shakespeare. He told his son to ask for a loan. If the son got the loan, then he should pay off his debt. Any money left over should be used to buy stockings at Evesham market for their shop. Quiney, staying at the Bell Inn in Carter Lane near St. Paul's Cathedral, wrote to Shakespeare on October 25 begging for his help.

> Loving Countryman, I am bold of you as a Friend, craving your help with xxxli—(£30, or about $48) . . . You shall Friend me much in helping me out of all the debts I owe in London. . . . You shall neither lose credit nor money by me . . . and if we bargain further you shall be paymaster yourself. . . My time bids me hasten to an end. . . I fear I shall not be back this night from the court. Haste. . . .

The letter was possibly not sent. It probably got mixed into Quiney's papers where it was preserved. Did Quiney bump into Shakespeare before he could send the letter? Or did Shakespeare return the letter with his reply?

Whatever happened to the letter, it appears that Shakespeare promised to help obtain the money. Sturley wrote to Quiney on November 4. He made a reference to a promise, but was looking for cash.

> . . . our countryman Mr Wm Shak, would procure us money, which I
> will like of as I shall hear when, and where. . . and how. . .

Quiney and Sturley appear to have approached Shakespeare. They thought he would have £30, around $48, available, or he would know where he could lay his hands on it. Shakespeare may well have taken the same line that he appears to have taken with Greene. He would not use his own money for the loan. Perhaps he distrusted their ability to repay. But on this occasion, Shakespeare uses contacts to see that his fellow townsmen would get their money.

In the end, though, Quiney's business at court was successful. His expenses were paid. These letters open a window on Shakespeare's business dealings. They show the strength of his connections with Stratford, where he was now a large property owner and an investor.

Shakespeare bought New Place in Stratford in May 1597. There had been several bad harvests that were pushing up grain prices. As always during such times of shortage, those who can afford to do so have a tendency to hoard what is in short supply. They keep themselves stocked up. They also wait until the shortage has pushed up prices so that they can sell what they have at a profit. In February 1598, a Stratford survey showed that William Shakespeare was hoarding ten quarters of malt. Malt is a grain used for brewing beer. Shakespeare's malt was worth about £25, or about $40. A laborer at this time could earn about 4 **shillings**, or about 32 cents, a week. Shakespeare had one of the larger stockpiles of malt in the town. Either he was holding the malt for his own home brewing or he was holding it to sell later at a profit. What is important is that he had enough spare cash to buy such an amount.

Around the time that The Globe began to open its doors to the paying public, Shakespeare moved from the London house he owned in St. Helen's parish. It was near The Theatre and The Curtain, but not close to the playhouses on the south bank of the river. He went to live in the **Liberty** of the Clink, near The Globe. Many of the **Lord Chamberlain's** Men seem to have made the same move. But it seems that Richard Burbage did not. When he died in 1619, he was still living in Holywell Street, near the original Theatre.

TWELFTH NIGHT

In early February 1602, a law student at the Middle Temple in London made this note in his diary. He was commenting on a feast held on Candlemas, the second day of February.

> we had a play called *Twelfth Night*, or *What You Will* A good practice to make the steward believe his lady was in love with him.

The play had probably been written sometime during 1601. It presents a wonderfully upside-down world. In the play, fools are wise and wise men fools. Girls are boys and nothing is quite what it seems. There is a serious frame to the play. The plot is set in motion by a shipwreck. One of the principal characters is in mourning. There is a cruel, unjust imprisonment near its end. But it is a much less troubled comedy than *As You Like It*.

Twelfth Night, which is January 6 and the last day of

the Christmas season, was a day of feasting and fooling. It was often led by a **Lord of Misrule**, who was a child or servant chosen to create disorder. *Twelfth Night* is a play about confusion and desire. It explores the gap between what people think they want and what they really want. It looks at the difference between who people think they are and who they really are.

A shipwrecked girl named Viola disguises herself as a boy called Cesario. She joins the court of Count Orsino. The Count is hopelessly in love with the Countess Olivia. Olivia is in mourning for her own dead brother. The Count sends Cesario with messages for Olivia. But, Olivia falls in love with Cesario, who is really the girl named Viola. Olivia has another suitor. He is Sir Andrew Aguecheek. He is being encouraged to pursue Olivia by her uncle, Sir Toby Belch. The steward responsible for running her household is Malvolio. He is a pompous **Puritan** who hates fun of every kind. Finally there is Feste. He is an "allowed fool." This means he has permission to tell the truth, however painful the truth might be.

Belch and his friends trick Malvolio into believing Olivia loves him. Malvolio makes a fool of himself and is locked up as a madman. Meanwhile, Viola's twin brother, Sebastian, turns up. He did not drown in the shipwreck. Olivia falls in love with him, because she thinks he is Cesario. Viola has now fallen in love with Orsino. In the end, as confusions are unraveled, the two couples, Olivia and Sebastian and Viola and Orsino, marry.

The play is full of light hearts and joy. But, as so often

is found in Shakespeare's plays, there are uncomfortable undercurrents. Both Olivia and Viola are mourning for their brothers. Olivia's mourning is so inward-looking that she has lost touch with reality. It takes a good dose of Feste's witty realism to help.

> The more fool, madonna, to mourn for your brother's
> soul, being in heaven. . .
>
> *Twelfth Night,* Act I Scene 5, lines 66–67

Viola is much more realistic. She decides on a plan for her own survival. Her grief is real, but she deals with it by dressing like her brother. They were twins and putting on boy's clothes makes her look like him.

This contrast between Olivia's self–love and Viola's love for another runs through the whole play. Olivia is proud and vain. Viola is witty, realistic, and generous in her attitude toward others. Although she is falling in love with Orsino, she continues to try to persuade Olivia to marry him. Another sharp contrast is Malvolio's high opinion of himself with Antonio's unselfishness. Antonio is a good friend to Sebastian and a remarkably unselfish friend. He tries to protect Sebastian, even though it puts him in great personal danger.

As an allowed fool, Feste shows far more wisdom and insight than the supposedly wise Malvolio, who is so easily taken in by Toby Belch and his friends.

Finally, the confusions of *Twelfth Night* focus on the uncertainties between boy and girl. Olivia loves Cesario, who is really a girl. She meets Sebastian and thinks he is Cesario. Viola loves Orsino, but because she is dressed as a boy, she cannot declare her love.

Although time and patience untangle the knots, there remain lingering uncertainties. How much did Orsino love the "boy" Cesario before he knew the "boy" was a girl? How much of the girl that Viola is hiding under the "boy" Cesario did Olivia fall in love with? How much do we all search for the "other half" to make us whole? This is an idea that Shakespeare had already explored in *The Comedy of Errors*. But in *Twelfth Night,* he takes the idea further. How far is each of us both male and female? It is an idea that modern psychology has endorsed, but the character Sebastian says it first.

> You are betrothed both to a maid and man
>
> *Twelfth Night,* Act 5 Scene 1, line 261

This ambivalence between man and woman gains even greater force for an audience, because in Shakespeare's time, boys played the parts of women. Shakespeare's audience was watching a girl—Viola—played by a boy, pretending to be a boy—Cesario—being loved by Olivia, a woman also played by a boy.

Near the end, Viola and Sebastian find one another at last. And not only are they united, but also Viola and Orsino, Olivia and Sebastian, Sebastian and Antonio, and even Sir Toby Belch and the servant Maria are all united. Here are so many different ways in which two separate beings can come together as a single loving whole. The confusions of *Twelfth Night* are over.

But the last word is with Feste, the fool who is also wise. Feste remains alone at the end of the play, singing a sad song. Indeed, his presence throughout adds the tones of autumn's dying leaves to the whole play. He has kept his wits, while all those around him are losing theirs. He understands, as he sings, that

> Present mirth hath present laughter.
> What's to come is still unsure. . .
> Youth's a stuff will not endure.'
>
> *Twelfth Night,* Act 2 Scene 3, lines 47–48, 51

HAMLET

Somewhere between 1600 and 1602, Shakespeare wrote what has become one of his most famous plays. When it was registered for printing, or at least to prevent anyone else from printing it, on July 26, 1602, it was called *The Revenge of Hamlet Prince of Denmark.* It first appeared in print a year later in a version that was probably based on the imperfect memory of an actor who had played a minor role in the play.

In 1604 a further edition claimed to present the play "according to the true and perfect copy." This edition was nearly twice as long as the first edition. It is likely that Shakespeare's own original text, or something like it, was used for the 1604 edition, but that the play was further revised in later performances. These later revisions formed the basis of the text in the First **Folio** edition of 1623. It was put together by Shakespeare's fellow actors several years after his death.

The play was first advertised as *The Revenge of Hamlet.* . . . This gives an important clue as to its style and meaning. Revenge as a subject is as old as drama itself and as modern as today's movies. Ancient Greek and Roman plays frequently use the drive to avenge the death of a parent or a child as the motive for action and the reason for conflict. The plays of Seneca, written in Rome in the first century, were very influential models for English **tragedy**. They include complex, highly theatrical, and extremely bloody deaths that are devised as a punishment for killing. Vendettas pass down from one generation to another. They are only resolved by general blood-letting to cleanse families or society of their guilt and to bring order out of chaos.

These plays were in fashion in the 1580s and 1590s. A version of *Hamlet*, probably not by Shakespeare, was performed from at least 1589 onward. Christopher Marlowe makes use of the revenge tradition in his play, *The Jew of Malta*. Thomas Kyd's *The Spanish Tragedy* was one of the most popular revenge plays. It included a ghost demanding vengeance, as well as a "pretend" play enacted by some of the characters within the main play. At the end, the stage is littered with dead bodies. These are all recognizable features of *Hamlet*. But Kyd's characters are actors in both senses of the word. They devise the most theatrical means of death possible for their enemies. They grasp the demand to kill with tremendous urgency.

Hamlet is set in the Danish castle of Elsinore. Hamlet's father, the king, has died. The king's widow, Gertrude, has married the old king's brother Claudius. Hamlet is unhappy about the speed of his mother's remarriage, which took place two months after his father's death. The ghost of the dead king appears to his son to tell him that he was killed by Claudius. He demands that Hamlet should revenge him. Also at Elsinore is a courtier called Polonius. Polonius has a son named Laertes, who leaves for France, and a daughter, named

Ophelia, who is in love with Hamlet. Hamlet pretends to be insane as part of his plan to revenge his father, and he rejects Ophelia. Polonius tries to find out what is affecting Hamlet. At the same time Claudius and Gertrude have encouraged Hamlet's old friends, Rosencrantz and Guildenstern, to also find out what is affecting Hamlet. But Hamlet will confide in no one.

When a band of traveling players arrive at the castle, Hamlet devises a plot to make Claudius tell the truth. Hamlet adds some new scenes to a play that the company is to perform before the king. The scenes act out the killing of Hamlet's own father. When Claudius sees the performance of the play, he panics. He arranges for Rosencrantz and Guildenstern to take Hamlet away to England and to have him murdered.

In the meantime, Hamlet has gone to see his mother, Gertrude, in her bedchamber. Polonius has been speaking with her before Hamlet arrives. He hides behind a large hanging tapestry. Hamlet tries to persuade his mother to give up Claudius. The ghost appears to Hamlet again, and Hamlet becomes more and more frenzied. Hearing a noise behind the tapestry, he lunges with his sword and kills Polonius.

Claudius is trapped between the demands of governing war-torn Denmark, Hamlet's behavior, and his own increasing guilt. Laertes returns when he hears of his father's death and swears revenge. Ophelia's grief makes her insane, and she drowns herself.

Hamlet escapes on the journey to England. He returns to Denmark aware of Claudius's intention to murder him. Claudius tries to bring matters to a close, and a duel is arranged between Hamlet and Laertes. Laertes' sword is to be tipped with poison. In addition, Claudius prepares a poisoned cup of wine for Hamlet. They fight, but things go wrong. Gertrude drinks the poisoned wine. In the confusion of the fight, Laertes and Hamlet are wounded with the poisoned sword. Just before he dies, Hamlet kills Claudius.

Shakespeare's *Hamlet* is a full-blooded revenge play with ghosts, plays-within-plays, the glint of flashing swords, and a good deal of blood. But this Hamlet is no actor rushing into vengeance. Rather, he is a man plagued with doubt and indecision. The characters of Kyd's play were often simply sketched in. Shakespeare draws his characters much more fully. Their complex motivation shows their own sense of guilt and anxiety. The desire for revenge is seen in the context of a tricky political situation. By a bitter irony, Hamlet bungles just about every killing he tries. Hearing a sound behind a curtain, he stabs not his uncle, but the old political adviser, Polonius. This sets up another revenge plot by Laertes and causes Ophelia's madness. Even the deaths at the end of the play are a mess.

The plot is full of accidents, delays, and mistakes—just like life. The full text of the 1604 edition is 3,300 lines long and lasts nearly four hours. These words are a breeding ground for doubt on the part of the actors. The words offer the characters opportunities for action. They also offer reasons for not acting.

> To be, or not to be; that is the question;
> Whether 'tis nobler in the mind to suffer
> The slings and arrows of outrageous fortune,
> Or to take arms against a sea of troubles,

> And, by opposing, end them. . .
> Thus conscience doth make cowards of us all,
> And thus the native hue of resolution
> Is sicklied o'er with the pale cast of thought
> And enterprises of great pith and moment
> With this regard their currents turn awry,
> And lose the name of action.
>
> *Hamlet,* Act 3 Scene 1, lines 58–62, 85–90

King Claudius is conscience-stricken by his killing of Hamlet's father. Hamlet worries about his own conscience before he does anything at all. Words, their meanings, and the way they are the springs of action continue to fascinate Hamlet. When the group of traveling players arrive at Elsinore, Hamlet marvels when one of them declaims a speech about the ancient Trojan war. The speech is full of intense emotion. But Hamlet's feelings cannot push him towards revenge.

> What would he do
> Had he the motive and the cue for passion
> That I have?. . . I . . .
> . . . can say nothing—no, not for a king
> Upon whose property and most dear life
> A damned defeat was made. . .
> O vengeance!—
> Why, what an ass am I? Ay, sure, this is most brave,
> That I, the son of the dear murderèd,
> Must, like a whore, unpack my heart with words
> And fall a-cursing like a very drab*. . .
>
> *Hamlet,* Act 2 Scene 2, lines 561–563, 566, 570–572, 583–588

Hamlet arranges for the players to act out a scene that

---

* drab = a prostitute

will "catch the conscience of the king." He succeeds up to a point, but the final acts of revenge come about through a different quarrel altogether. None of Hamlet's words have led to actions that will properly avenge the killing of the old king. In the end nothing has worked, and Hamlet, the man most able to express his feelings but able to do precious little with them, dies inarticulately.

> The rest is silence
> O, O, O, O.

Hamlet, Act 5 Scene 2, lines 310–311

If Shakespeare was writing or revising *Hamlet* in about 1601, then there is particular poignancy about Hamlet's grief for his father's death. This is the year that Shakespeare's own father, John Shakespeare, died in Stratford. The death of his father made William considerably richer. The terms of John Shakespeare's will are not known, but as the eldest son, William would have received a large inheritance of land and property. And is it entirely coincidental that the Prince of Denmark's name, Hamlet, is similar to Shakespeare's own son's name, Hamnet, who had died four years earlier? The Prince's name goes back into legend, but the similarity with his dead son's name may have attracted Shakespeare to the subject.

THE DEVELOPMENT OF INDOOR THEATERS

If the tradition of outdoor theaters had grown out of the open-air performances of the **Corpus Christi** plays, then there was another equally important tradition of indoor performances. Playing companies had regularly performed in the halls of great houses, as well as in the market or guild halls of towns, such as Stratford. There was also a long tradition of performing in the halls of schools and universities, as well as in royal palaces.

It should come as no surprise, then, that in 1576, the first outdoor London playhouse, The Theatre, was built, and the first permanent indoor playhouse was established. The indoor playhouse was in the converted monastic buildings at the Blackfriars. This was located on the north bank of the Thames River not far from St. Paul's Cathedral.

This playhouse was set up for a company of **boy players** under the direction of Richard Farrant. Farrant at that time was Master of the Children of the Chapel Royal, which provided the choir for the queen's services in her palaces, as they still do today. Farrant established his playhouse under false pretenses. He obtained the rooms in the Blackfriars by saying that they were to be used as a school. But in fact the rooms were converted into a playhouse. Farrant was aware that there was money to be made from theatrical performances. So he used the fact that acting was an important part of Elizabethan education to turn his boys into a professional company. Farrant was thrown out of the Blackfriars in 1584 when his landlord, William More, realized what was going on.

Boy players continued to be a significant part of the London playgoing scene. It seems unlikely that Shakespeare himself ever wrote for them. If some of his comments in *Hamlet* are anything to go by, he maybe didn't think much of their abilities. But boy players did attract many other leading playwrights.

However, not many boys went on to become professional adult actors. However, Nathan Field, who had been with the Children of the Chapel Royal from about 1600, joined the King's Men by 1616. He became one of its leading players. His father was a **Puritan** clergyman who preached against plays and players.

It is known that the **Lord Chamberlain's** Men were allowed to use the Cross Keys Inn in Gracechurch Street during the winter of 1598. It is probable that rooms inside other inns were also used from time to time for performances by different companies. Before this, in 1596, James Burbage was looking around for an indoor theater. Like Richard Farrant, he settled for the Blackfriars. He negotiated with William More for the lease of another part of the old buildings. He was interested in one of the halls. Like modern developments in London Docklands or today's loft apartments in former factories, the old Blackfriars monastery had become a fashionable place to live.

Perhaps Burbage hoped his indoor theater would attract customers who did not like the cold and wet of an outdoor theater, or customers who did not like attending theater with the less fashionable playgoers of the outdoor playhouses. Whatever his reasons, he did not take into consideration those who might oppose his plans.

Their **patron,** Henry Carey, may have been involved in Burbage's plans. He certainly owned property in the Blackfriars. But after his death, the wealthy families in the Blackfriars, including their late patron, George Carey, the second Lord Hunsdon, petitioned the government to refuse a license. Any advantage in bringing a playhouse to the Blackfriars was offset by the fact that it would inevitably bring noisy players and even noisier—and probably **plague**-ridden—playgoers, too. Those opposed to the playhouse were also worried that the playhouse would increase traffic congestion. This is a familiar objection even today. Their objections were sustained. Burbage's playhouse did not go into the Blackfriars.

Burbage's plan to attract a different audience had backfired. However, his converted building was used as a playhouse. For the next few years the boy company, the Children of the Chapel Royal—also known as the Children of the Revels—were allowed to return. They played there in competition with the boys of St. Paul's, who had a hall nearer to the Cathedral.

In 1608, the **boy players'** companies suddenly collapsed in the teeth of **Puritan** opposition. The Blackfriars became available. This time the King's Men moved in with little opposition. Old father Burbage's wish to see a permanent indoor playhouse had become a reality.

THE BLACKFRIARS THEATRE

There is scholarly argument as to whether moving into an indoor theater made any difference to the type of plays the King's Men put on, or to their performance style. First, players had always worked inside as well as out. They played inside when on tour and at court. Second, the companies never got rid of the outdoor theaters. Those theaters were bigger, and therefore earned them more money. They were a significant part of the style of performing, and they were cheaper to run. The candles for lighting the indoor theaters were costly. Third, the crucial steps in the development of a new type of play and a new, intense performing style had already been taken before 1608. However, the intimacy of the indoor playhouses and their opportunity for different special effects, such as candlelight and the sense of enclosure, widened the range of what was written and how it could be played.

OTHELLO

From about 1602, Shakespeare's plays become increasingly compressed. He no longer spreads plots across different layers of society. Instead, he looks more directly at the hidden springs of action in the relationships of small groups of people. The comedy is often bitter and cynical. The view of the world that the plays present is frequently savage. This trend reached a climax with *King Lear,* which developed from typically Shakespearean themes of love, friendship, separation and loss, betrayal and revenge, and the gap between words and actions. In Shakespeare's play *Othello,* these themes are in their tightest focus.

Othello is the story of a north African Moor who has become a famous soldier by leading Venice in its war against the Turks. He is tricked by his ensign, Iago, who is a junior officer acting as Othello's personal assistant. Iago gets Othello to falsely believe that Othello's wife, Desdemona, is having an affair with a soldier named Cassio. Othello becomes very jealous. In the end Othello kills Desdemona. Only then, too late, does he learn the truth, and he kills himself.

The strength of the play comes from Shakespeare's dissection of the hidden motives and emotions that drive people to action. But he overturns our expectations in a number of ways. First, the general, Othello, is a Moor. Just as with Shylock the Jew in *The Merchant of Venice*, Shakespeare takes someone his audience would regard with suspicion and fear and shows his basic humanity. Othello is, like King Lear, a man "more sinned against, than sinning." Neither Othello's jealous rages, nor his bravery are to be attributed to the fact that he is a Moor. Not that Shakespeare ignores the question of prejudice. Desdemona's father, Brabanzio, can have his racism unlocked by Iago.

> Even now, now, very now, an old black ram
> Is tupping your white ewe. Arise, arise!
> Awake the snorting citizens with the bell,
> Or else the devil will make a grandsire of you.
>
> *Othello*, Act I Scene I, lines 88–91

Othello's jealous response is perhaps more easily unlocked because of the Moor's anxiety that he is different, that Desdemona may prefer another, and that he does not understand her.

Shakespeare overturns our expectations in another way, too. When writing *Othello*, he was contributing to a fashion for **tragedies**, which explore the inner motives of men and women. In part, tragedies develop the revenge tradition. They are generally set in Italy, and involve sexual adventures or threatened loss of innocence. They frequently invoke madness, but generally make clear why the characters act as they do. They tend to have a wicked manipulator who unleashes suffering onto innocent victims.

But generally there are reasons, however twisted, for what the characters do. In *Othello*, Shakespeare presents us with a motiveless manipulator. Iago offers many reasons why he is out to get Othello. None of the reasons seems strong. Near the beginning of the play, he admits to himself and the audience that he "hates the Moor," and that is sufficient motivation. At the end, he gives reasons for his actions.

> Demand me nothing. What you know, you know.
> From this time forth I never will speak word.
>
> *Othello,* Act 5 Scene 2, lines 309–310

The heart of the play is a disturbing emptiness. The innocence of Desdemona and Othello is destroyed for no other reason than hatred. Othello descends into jealousy. His deep and energetic emotions have been unlocked for no reason at all. By stating his intent at the beginning, Iago makes the play one long exercise in **dramatic irony**. This reaches its climax in the great scene, Act 3 Scene 3, in which he finally traps Othello in his net and turns the general into a raging, vengeful man. The audience knows that Iago is tricking Othello and lying about Desdemona and Cassio. But the audience can do nothing about it except to secretly admire his manipulative skills, pity the deceived Moor, and fear for Desdemona. The audience watches as the swirling waters of jealousy sweep away Othello.

> Like to the Pontic Sea,
> Whose icy current and compulsive course
> Ne'er knows retiring ebb, but keeps due on
> To the Propontic and the Hellespont,
> Even so my bloody thoughts with violent pace
> Shall ne'er look back, ne'er ebb to humble love,
> Till that a capable and wide revenge
> Swallow them up.
>
> *Othello,* Act 3 Scene 3, lines 456–463

IN THE FORTY-FIFTH YEAR OF HIS AGE

From before 1604, Shakespeare had moved back north of the river, away from The Globe. He was living in the parish of St. Olave. He had lodgings in Silver Street, which was a respectable part of the city. It was an area now bounded by Moorgate and Poultry. Shakespeare's landlord at this time was Christopher Mountjoy. He was a Frenchman engaged in the fashionable trade of making tires. Tires are headpieces for ladies that are ornamented with gold, silver, and jewels. What happened next gives a rare glimpse into Shakespeare's world and the daily life of London.

In 1604, one of Mountjoy's former **apprentices**, Stephen Belott, started working for Shakespeare again. The Mountjoys soon began to encourage Stephen to marry their daughter Mary. Shakespeare appears to have been called in to help persuade Stephen. The couple were married on November 19, 1604, in St. Olave's Church down the road from the Mountjoys'.

Christopher Mountjoy clearly expected Stephen and Mary to stay and help with the business, but, to his annoyance, they moved out and began their own business nearby. Belott believed that he had been promised a cash dowry as part of the marriage settlement and a further £200, about $320, when old Mountjoy died. All the newlyweds got as a dowry was £10, or about $16 and a few pieces of secondhand household items. After Mrs. Mountjoy died in 1606, the Belotts returned to Silver Street. They became partners in the business, but there were more arguments. Within a few years they left again. By

1612, anxious that old Mountjoy was going to cut them out of his will, they went to court.

It was then that Stephen Belott, backed by various friends and former servants of Mountjoy's, recalled Shakespeare's part in the affair. Shakespeare had repeated Mountjoy's promise to give Belott money if he married Mary. Shakespeare, who had moved out years earlier, was called to give evidence. Either he could not or would not remember exactly what had been said or promised. The matter fizzled out. It was decided that neither Mountjoy nor Belott were up to much. Shakespeare returned to his own business.

Although Shakespeare lived in London for at least part of the years from the early 1590s, it is unlikely that his wife Anne and his children ever joined him. Until he bought New Place, they almost certainly lived at the Shakespeare family home on Henley Street in Stratford. Shakespeare gradually increased the amount of land and property he owned in the town. On May 1, 1602, he purchased 170 acres of land from William and John Combe. The land was scattered in small parcels around the north and east of Stratford. He paid £320, or about $500, for the land. This was a very considerable sum, which may have come partly from his inheritance from his father, who had died the year before.

Three years later, Shakespeare bought a 33-year interest in Stratford's tithes. Tithes were originally the church's right to receive a tenth part of the agricultural produce of a parish. Tithes provided the local priest with a living. In Stratford, these had been paid to the priests of Holy Trinity Church. After this religious foundation was dissolved in the mid-1500s, the tithes passed to the **borough** of Stratford. The borough then sold the right to collect the tithes to private individuals. In turn, they paid a fixed sum each year back to the borough. But the private individuals kept the profits.

It was a part of this arrangement that Shakespeare bought in 1605. He paid £440, or about $700. In three years he had at least $1,200 with which to dispose. Or was he rearranging the income available from his inheritance? The gross income from the tithes was about $100 a year. A repayment of $27 a year was made to the borough. Another Stratford resident who retained an interest in the tithes received £5, or $8. This left Shakespeare with about $64 a year profit. By about 1613, he would have gotten back the £440 he had originally paid. He and his descendants had another 21 years to enjoy the profits. This was likely a total of over £800, or $1,300. Already in 1602 Shakespeare was clearly planning for his own and his children's future.

In June 1607, Shakespeare's eldest daughter, Susanna, married Dr. John Hall. Dr. Hall provided medical treatment to many local families. The Halls continued to live in Stratford. Their daughter, Elizabeth, was born in February 1608. In August 1607, William Shakespeare's nephew, Edward, the illegitimate son of his brother Edmund, was buried in St. Giles-without-Cripplegate's cemetery in London. Four months later, at the turn of the year, brother Edmund, who was also a player, died. Then in September 1608, William's mother, Mary, died in Stratford. The theaters were closed for much of 1608 because of **plague**. Either Shakespeare or someone on his or the King's Men's behalf made use of this down time. This is when a number of the plays were printed.

By 1608, when he was 44 years old, William Shakespeare was a wealthy property owner in Stratford. He continued to be a businessman with interests in the London playhouses. He was also an experienced man of the theater working with the King's Men, the company who had received King James I's own special license. His plays were known at court and in the popular public playhouses. They were performed both outdoors at The Globe and indoors at the Blackfriars. Many of his plays were published in individual editions, as were the poems *Venus and Adonis* and *The Rape of Lucrece*. Now, two more printed books appeared that contained some of his most complex, profound, and puzzling writing. They were *King Lear* in 1608 and the 154 *Sonnets* in 1609.

KING LEAR

The story of King Lear and his three daughters was well-known at the beginning of the 1600s. There was even a play on the subject published in 1605. It provided Shakespeare with much of his plot. Shakespeare's own *The History of King Lear* was printed in 1608 in a **Quarto** edition. This may have been the text of the version performed before King James on December 26, 1606. However, a substantially changed text was published in the **Folio** in 1623. It is likely that these changes were the result of the experience of performing the play over a number of years.

The story of King Lear belongs to a world not far

removed from a fairy tale. A king decides to divide his kingdom between his three daughters. Before they can claim their shares, he asks them to say how much they love him. The two eldest, Goneril and Regan, flatter him suitably and get their reward, But the third daughter, Cordelia, refuses to join in. This is not because she does not love her father, but because she finds the demand abhorrent.

Lear: What can you say to win a third more opulent
Than your sisters?

Cordelia: Nothing, my lord.

Lear: How? Nothing can come of nothing. Speak again.

Cordelia: Unhappy that I am, I cannot heave
My heart into my mouth. I love your majesty
According to my bond, nor more nor less.

The History of King Lear, Act I Scene I, lines 79–85

Lear is furious and throws her out. In contrast, however, one of her suitors, the King of France, still wishes to marry her because he loves her.

One of Lear's nobles, the Duke of Gloucester, has two sons, Edmund and Edgar. Edmund is illegitimate and harbors a grudge against his brother, who will inherit everything. He sets a plot in motion to make Gloucester think Edgar is planning to kill him. This gets Edgar banished. In the meantime, Lear has divided his kingdom between Goneril and Regan. He intends to spend his time equally with the two of them. But the women and their husbands plot to take all Lear's power away. As they turn against him, he goes insane. He is driven out into the stormy countryside where he calls down curses on himself and begs nature to destroy the whole world. Edgar, who is pretending to be insane to escape his brother, meets Lear and takes him in from the storm.

But Gloucester has fallen into the clutches of Goneril, Regan, and his wicked son, Edmund. They tear out Gloucester's eyes and send him, too, out into the world. Gloucester makes his way to the cliffs of Dover to kill himself, but Edgar finds him. He pretends to help Gloucester jump from the cliff, but in fact saves his life.

A war has been declared between France and Britain. Cordelia is with the French army, but she is captured by Edmund and Lear, who is sane again but old and mentally fragile. Lear begs his daughter's forgiveness, and they are reconciled. Goneril and Regan have both fallen in love with Edmund. But Edmund quarrels with them and Goneril's husband, Albany, who is beginning to sicken of the plotting. Now Edgar arrives and challenges Edmund to a duel. They fight and Edmund is defeated. Goneril and Regan both take poison. An order goes out to save Lear and Cordelia, whom Edmund had condemned to execution. But it is too late. Cordelia is hanged. Lear, with his youngest daughter dead, dies of grief and despair. Albany and Edgar remain to establish good order in the kingdom.

> **Albany:** The weight of this sad time we must obey,
> Speak what we feel, not what we ought to say.
> The oldest have borne most. We that are young
> Shall never see so much, or live so long.
>
> *The History of King Lear,* Scene 24, lines 318–321.
> (In *The Tragedy of King Lear* [the Folio text] this speech is given
> to Edgar: Act 5 Scene 3, lines 299–302.)

For many people, *King Lear* is one of Shakespeare's

greatest plays. It is at once huge in its scope, yet often intensely intimate in its feel. It would have been at home in the great outdoor playhouse and on the candlelit indoor stage at the Blackfriars. It is a deeply serious and thrilling exploration of fundamental moral, psychological, and spiritual questions. No summary can do it justice.

To perform, watch, or read this play is to be plunged deep into the paradoxes of life. Nowhere is the gap wider between how people appear and how people are. The play swings between the poles of sanity and madness, words and silence, sight and blindness, folly and wisdom. Its main figure is a king. His actions and his foolishness have wide consequences for others. He is also a father, and his relationship with his daughters is central. Lear misunderstands Goneril and Regan. What they appear is not what they are. He realizes the truth too late. He misunderstands Cordelia, too. She can say nothing, because she cannot lie. She loves her father as much as she can. The nature of truth, the difficulty of telling the truth, and the painfulness of the truth's consequences run through the play alongside an exploration of what it means for one person to truly love another. Serious character flaws of vanity and lack of good judgement cause havoc. But in the character of Edmund, there is also calculating evil at work for which there is little motivation.

In *King Lear*, Shakespeare draws together many of the oppositions he has explored before. The intense charge of the play in performance comes from an almost fairy tale simplicity in the storytelling. Shakespeare would have known an ancient Greek definition that speaks of **tragedy**. It says tragedy awakens terror and pity as we watch the fall of a great hero, but it also offers us change and redemption at the end. The final, hopeful lines of *King Lear* remind the audience of the cost of the redemption.

SONNETS AND A LOVER'S COMPLAINT

In 1598, Francis Meres, in his book *Palladis Tamia, Wit's Treasury* remarked that

> the sweet witty soul of Ovid lives in mellifluous and honey-tongued *Shakespeare*, witness his *Venus and Adonis*, his *Lucrece*, his sugared Sonnets among his private friends . . .

Meres praises Shakespeare for his plays as well, but the reference to "sugared Sonnets" raises a number of questions. The sonnet is a 14-line rhymed verse form. It was very popular in the 1590s. Shakespeare himself mocks the desire of anyone who was in love to compose a few sonnets in *Love's Labour's Lost*. Yet he has his lovers speak in sonnet-form at one point in *Romeo and Juliet*. A couple of sonnets by Shakespeare were printed in 1599. But it was not until 1609 that a sequence of 154 sonnets was published under his name. Were these composed when sonnet sequences were in fashion ten years earlier? Did Meres know the collection when he referred to sonnets known among Shakespeare's "private friends?"

If so, why did Shakespeare not publish them when they might have made him some money and raised his prestige? The other possibility is that sonnets written in a less ordered fashion at that time were reworked into a sequence immediately before 1609. The earlier poems were written when the playhouses were closed during the plague. Did Shakespeare make use of another enforced lay-off in 1608 to rework, and maybe add to, a collection of earlier poems?

This is only one of the many puzzles of the *Sonnets*. The sequence appears to tell the story of a triangular relationship between a poet, a young man, and a woman. Scholars and critics have enjoyed trying to find the identities of these people. It is assumed that Shakespeare himself was the poet. They have also looked for incidents in and around Shakespeare's life that might have prompted the poems. It is safe to say that no one has come up with a completely persuasive argument. This also encourages more speculation.

One thing that is clear is that the sequence of 154 sonnets is highly unconventional. At times it almost seems to mock the earlier poets' practice of using the sequence to praise a woman's beauty. Many are addressed to a man with whom the poet himself seems to be in love. Many of the sonnets addressed to a woman are not flattering, although the poet claims to praise and love her.

> My mistress' eyes are nothing like the sun;
> Coral is far more red than her lips' red.
> If snow be white, why then her breasts are dun;
> If hairs be wires, black wires grow on her head. . .
>> And yet, by heaven, I think my love as rare
>> As any she belied with false compare.
>
> *Sonnet 130, lines 1–4, 13–14*

The years before 1608 were a time when Shakespeare appeared to be at his most cynical about love and human relationships. This is the time of the sexual bitterness of *Troilus and Cressida*, the emptiness of

SHAKE-SPEARES

SONNETS.

Neuer before Imprinted.

AT LONDON
By *G. Eld* for *T. T.* and are
to be folde by *Iohn Wright*, dwelling
at Chrift Church gate.
1609.

TO.THE.ONLIE.BEGETTER.OF.
THESE.INSVING.SONNETS.
Mʳ. W. H. ALL.HAPPINESSE.
AND.THAT.ETERNITIE.
PROMISED.

BY.

OVR.EVER-LIVING.POET.

WISHETH.

THE.WELL-WISHING.
ADVENTVRER.IN.
SETTING.
FORTH.

T. T.

These pages show the title and dedication for the 1609 edition of Shakespeare's *Sonnets*. These pages can be viewed at The Shakespeare Birthplace Trust, Stratford-upon-Avon.

155

Othello, and the tragic depths of *King Lear. Pericles, Prince of Tyre,* a play Shakespeare wrote at about the same time as the *Sonnets,* has significant scenes in a **brothel,** as does *Measure for Measure* a year or two earlier. Seen from this perspective, the intense emotional pain of the *Sonnets* begins to fit into Shakespeare's dramatic concerns. This has led some scholars to see the sequence of sonnets not as autobiographical, but as a fictional exploration of despair and loss.

Certainly this also helps make some sense of the other poem attached to the sequence in the printed edition of 1609. *A Lover's Complaint* is a 329-line poem in seven-line verses. It is very like the long, earlier poem, *The Rape of Lucrece,* which is also in seven-line verses and couched as a great lament for lost innocence. Many scholars now believe that *A Lover's Complaint* is intended to complete the sequence. They believe that it is meant to express, as did the lament of Lucrece, the outcome of the events expressed in the sonnets from the woman's point of view.

> When he most burned in heart-wished luxury,
> He preached pure maid and praised cold chastity. . .
> O that sad breath his spongy lungs bestowed,
> O all that borrowed motion seeming owed
> Would yet again betray the fore-betrayed,
> And new pervert a reconcilèd maid.
>
> *A Lover's Complaint,* lines 314–315, 326–329

FAIRY TALES

Although the style and subject matter of Shakespeare's plays change through his career, they do so only gradually and with a good deal of overlap. Plays on subjects drawn from ancient Greece and Rome span Shakespeare's whole career from *Titus Andronicus* at the beginning through *Julius Caesar* and the bitter *Troilus and Cressida,* and on to *Antony and Cleopatra* and *Coriolanus.* The victorious Mark Antony of *Julius Caesar* has become, in the later play, a man infatuated with the beautiful Queen of Egypt. He is torn between the queen and the conflicting claims of Roman duty. *Coriolanus* picks up the conflict between public duty and private desire, although from a very different angle. It is severely simple where *Antony and Cleopatra* is full of sensual imagery. Coriolanus's arrogant egotism is in stark contrast to Antony's wavering and uncertain path towards death.

From about 1606 onward, however, Shakespeare began to explore a new way of writing plays. He draws increasingly on magic for its effects. He delicately overlaps tragedy and comedy. These plays have some of the qualities of the best fairy tales in which we can face our deeper anxieties about loss, or the changes of growing up and getting older. As in fairy tales, good triumphs over evil. These plays are sometimes referred to as romances.

In *All's Well That Ends Well,* probably written about 1605, the King of France is cured of a chronic illness by a young woman named Helen. Helen substitutes herself to Bertram, whom she loves, for another woman he is trying to seduce, thus shaming him into marrying her. *Pericles, Prince of Tyre,* a very popular play at the time, was first printed in a Quarto in 1609. But it was omitted from the Folio, probably because it was known to have been written with George Wilkins. It is a romantic tale that takes its hero, Pericles, through as many adventures as any Hollywood movie. Finally he is healed of his suffering by his daughter, Marina, whom he had thought to be dead.

The relationship between fathers and daughters, painfully examined in *King Lear*, is at the heart of *The Winter's Tale*. This is a story based on one by Robert Greene, Shakespeare's old enemy of 1592. Jealous King Leontes wrongly accuses his wife, Hermione, of adultery. He imprisons her and arranges for their new-born daughter to be left to die on a distant seashore. Hermione pretends to be dead, but actually hides away for many years.

In the meantime, the child, who has been saved by shepherds and named Perdita, grows up and falls in love with Florizel. Florizel is the son of the man whom Leontes had accused of the affair with Hermione. Perdita and Florizel return to Leontes. Seeing her again, his stubborn heart melts. They go to the place where Leontes has been told there is a statue of his dead wife. He sees the statue and marvels at its lifelikeness. He is told that it is a special statue and can move. But he has been tricked. This is the real Hermione. In a moment of transformation, he finds his wife, his daughter, and himself. The play ends with Leontes asking their forgiveness and blessing.

Cymbeline, written in 1610 or 1611, takes the romantic fairy tale style further. It is a play of intertwined tragedy and comedy set in ancient Britain. The heroine Imogen dresses as a boy to seek her lover. He has landed with an invading army to avoid the loutish Cloten, son of her wicked stepmother. Cloten pursues her and is killed. Imogen, also thought to be dead, is laid beside him. She wakes to find a headless corpse. The wicked queen and stepmother dies. Imogen and her lover are united. Peace is restored.

THE TEMPEST

The first recorded performance of *The Tempest* was on November 1, 1611. The story is based on three sources. One is the accounts of a shipwreck published in 1610. The second is an essay on cannibals by the French thinker Michel de Montaigne, which was published in a famous English translation in 1603. The third source is the stories from Ovid's *Metamorphoses*. It is a play full of allusions to magic and to the new discoveries of the Americas. New worlds are in collision with the old.

Many years before the play begins, Prospero, a magician and former Duke of Milan, had been overthrown by his brother Antonio. Prospero was cast adrift in a boat with his daughter Miranda. The island on which they land is deserted, except for Caliban and his mother, Sycorax, who is a witch. Prospero imprisons Sycorax in a tree, where she dies. He then takes Caliban as his servant. Prospero releases Ariel, another spirit, from the same prison tree where he had been imprisoned by Sycorax. Ariel also becomes his servant. They all live on the island as Miranda grows up.

Prospero's brother Antonio is on a ship with other nobles. This includes Alonso, the King of Naples; Alonso's son Ferdinand; and various servants. Using his magic and seeking revenge, Prospero makes Ariel stir up a storm. All are shipwrecked on Prospero's island. Ferdinand meets Miranda and they fall in love. But Prospero tests Ferdinand by various ordeals. The nobles are enchanted and sleep, but two servants,

Stephano and Trinculo, meet Caliban. Caliban offers to be their servant. The three servants get drunk and Caliban offers to make Stephano and Trinculo lords of the island by overthrowing Prospero, and taking Miranda for themselves. Their plans fail. Miranda marries Ferdinand. Prospero abandons his plan for revenge and seeks to be reconciled with Antonio, who says nothing. Caliban is given back his island, and Ariel is set free. But the plot has been responsible for a further darkening of the mood. Once more, there is no simple, happy ending.

There is no reason to think that Shakespeare intended this to be his final play. He wrote or had a hand in at least three more plays. Nevertheless, *The Tempest* brings together many different ideas and elements from all his previous work. Many of these are expressed through the telling opposition of dark or angry magic and light or peaceable magic.

Sycorax is a practitioner of angry magic. At times, Prospero seems to share in these arts. He is angry with his brother and shows anger towards Ferdinand, Ariel, and Caliban. But Prospero also understands the power of peaceable magic as a cure that creates order. Ariel is the agent of this magic. Even though Prospero whips up the tempest that brings about the shipwreck, the storm is part of the process of cure. It is the means of establishing order. Prospero clearly states that all the crew and passengers are unharmed.

Magic is expressed in ritual. Prospero's magic staff helps conjure up the storm. It is what he breaks when he says farewell to magic at the end. Shakespeare also ritualizes magic through the use of a masque at the wedding banquet. This is a clear reference to court entertainment. It is also an opportunity to bring the gods on stage in the person of Jupiter in order to add to the theatrical spectacle.

The island is a place where appearances and reality can be confused. Nothing is what it seems. But at the same time, as in all the best fairy tales, the gap between what appears to be and what is true is closed. Towards the end is one of the few stage directions that Shakespeare included in his plays.

> [The nobles] *all enter the circle which Prospero had made, and there stand charmed; which Prospero observing, speaks. . .*

Prospero speaks words of forgiveness. They are not sentimental words, but words with a tough awareness of the pain their actions had caused him. He is still "the wrongèd Duke of Milan."

The gap between appearance and reality also has a part to play in the attitude toward Caliban, who was the original owner of the island. Although clearly meant to represent our lower, animal nature, Shakespeare nevertheless treats Caliban with a good deal of sympathy. Caliban may be smelly, he may lust after Miranda, he may be out for Prospero's blood, but he too has had his kingdom taken away, just as Prospero had lost Milan. Caliban is even allowed insight into the true nature of the isle.

> The isle is full of noises,
> Sounds, and sweet airs, that give delight and hurt not.
>
> *The Tempest*, Act 3 Scene 2, lines 138–139

As Prospero returns to Milan, Caliban gets his island back, and Ariel is released into the air. Although they seem opposites, there are some telling resemblances between Prospero the usurped magician, Caliban the enslaved dreamer, and the witch Sycorax.

The *Metamorphoses* of Ovid is a key text for Shakespeare. He would have read it at school. It provides him not only with sources for some of his plays, but also with the key ideas of transformation and resemblance that run through so much of his work. In Book 7, Ovid tells the story of the witch Medea. Shakespeare uses the description of her powerful witchcraft to describe some of the powers of Sycorax. He uses this description again at the end of the play when Prospero uses his magic to create the charmed circle in which the nobles will be trapped, then released, and finally forgiven. After an invocation of the spirit world that owes much to Ovid, and that shows how Prospero's "rough magic" connects with that of witchcraft, the magician turns his back on such things. He calls down "heavenly music" and vows to

> break my staff,
> Bury it certain fathoms in the earth,
> And deeper than did ever plummet sound
> I'll drown my book.

The Tempest, Act 5 Scene 1, lines 54–56

The gap between appearance and reality is often a source of suspicion in Shakespeare's writing. There is much suspicion in *The Tempest*, as well as Caliban's naive misreading of the drunken servants. But it is also the stuff of magic and is a key idea in the *Metamorphoses* of Ovid. For Ovid, the gap can be closed by love. There is no doubt that Shakespeare invites us to consider the same possibility. Love had closed the gap between people in *King Lear,* but not before the tragedy had overwhelmed fathers and children. Love brings together Pericles and Marina. Leontes touches the "statue" of his wife and finds her and his daughter again. He says,

> O, she's warm!
> If this be magic, let it be an art
> Lawful as eating.

The Winter's Tale, Act 5 Scene 3, lines 109–111

But it is, more simply and with more humanity, the magic of love that has waited for the right moment to bring forgiveness and reconciliation. So, too, in *The Tempest,* Prospero leaves magic behind and embraces the same love that has waited for the right moment to be reconciled.

> Now my charms are all o'erthrown
> And what strength I have's mine own,
> Which is most faint.

The Tempest, Epilogue, lines 1–2

11
WILL AND DEATH

In April and May 1611, the King's Men performed *Macbeth, Cymbeline,* and *The Winter's Tale* at The Globe playhouse in London. On September 11, in Stratford, a list was made of possible people who would contribute money for the upkeep of the local roads. Someone added Shakespeare's name in the margin. This was done possibly because he was not actually living in Stratford at the time, although his wife was presumably a resident in New Place. It is not known whether Shakespeare ever made the hoped for contribution.

The names on the Stratford list are in order of seniority within the town. It is significant that Shakespeare's name was added just below those of the **bailiff, alderman,** and steward. The steward is the town's official legal representative. Shakespeare's name appears above the "gentlemen." It is even above the name of his son-in-law Dr. John Hall. Shakespeare was high up in Stratford's pecking order, even if he was frequently away in London.

He may have been in Stratford on February 3, 1612, when his younger brother Gilbert was buried at Holy Trinity Church. Gilbert seems to have continued the family business in Stratford and to have been unmarried when he died. We know that Shakespeare was back in London on May 11 when he gave evidence in the Mountjoy case. At this hearing he was referred to as being "from Stratford." This may mean that he had no permanent London address to offer to the court. He did not attend the second hearing on June 19. Perhaps he returned to Stratford, or perhaps he was no longer needed in court. It is unlikely that he was in Stratford in February 1613 when his last surviving brother, Richard, died. The King's Men were busy preparing for the wedding of King James's daughter Elizabeth to Count Frederick V, Elector Palatine of the Rhine. The wedding took place on February 14 of that year.

THE TWO NOBLE KINSMEN

James's eldest son, Henry, had died in November 1612 after a painful illness. He was a favorite of his father, and he was looked upon as a king in the great traditions of honor and chivalry. The grief when he died was immense. It touched every aspect of society. The wedding of his sister Elizabeth, just a few months later, meant that grief had to be set aside. During the celebrations, the royal family saw *Much Ado About Nothing, Cardenio, The Winter's Tale, The Tempest,* and *Philaster. Cardenio* is a play by Shakespeare and his colleague John Fletcher. Fletcher was beginning to replace Shakespeare as resident playwright for the King's Men. The play is now lost. *Philaster* was written by Fletcher and Francis Beaumont.

All of these plays bring together pain and sadness, death and joy, and funerals and weddings. Shakespeare, once again with John Fletcher, and probably with Francis Beaumont, too, may have offered a new play. This play swung between the two poles of celebration and lament. It was *The Two Noble Kinsmen.*

The play casts doubt on the sentimental tradition that Shakespeare was somehow "bidding farewell to the stage" with *The Tempest*. It is a wonderful, complex, and deeply moving exploration of human life. It shows the painfully difficult and sometimes disturbingly funny attempts to make sense of it. The search for order never ends, but it is doomed to failure.

The Two Noble Kinsmen is based on a story by the medieval English poet Geoffrey Chaucer. Shakespeare never tries to hide this. In fact he seems to want us to see that he and Chaucer have the same perspective on the **tragicomedy** that is human life.

A month after the death of his brother Gilbert, and the marriage of Princess Elizabeth, Shakespeare bought a house in the Blackfriars close to the King's Men's indoor playhouse. It was also near to the river where he could be ferried across to The Globe. Shakespeare paid £140, or about $225, for the property. He put down a $130–cash deposit with a six-month period to raise the other $95. The present day Ireland's Yard, between Ludgate Circus and Queen Victoria Street east of Blackfriars railway station, is just south of the location of Shakespeare's property.

In the negotiations for the purchase of the property, Shakespeare is again described as from Stratford. It is not known if Shakespeare ever lived in this house, or even if he intended to.

ALL IS TRUE

During the spring of 1613, Shakespeare was working on another new play. It was based on the divorce of Catherine of Aragon from King Henry VIII. It was called *All is True*. Unfortunately, it is rarely performed today. The play explores many of the most distinctive

Shakespearean moments that have recurred throughout his 30 year writing career.

Henry VIII is shown as a great manipulator. He is a man who knows that the theatrical display of power is the best way to keep power. Tragic Queen Catherine is shown sewing, mending, and speaking simply but eloquently when put on trial. This is in contrast to the pomp and show of Henry and his courtiers. Her simplicity speaks more loudly than all of Henry's inflated language and presence. Cardinal Wolsey, as he falls from power, also shifts his language to the simple and direct.

> I have ventured
> Like little wanton boys that swim on bladders,
> This many summers in a sea of glory,
> But far beyond my depth . . .
>
> *All is True*, Act 3 Scene 2, lines 359–362

There is no sense here that Shakespeare is losing his grip as he gets older. The plotting, the language, and the dramatic tension are maintained throughout the play. It ends with a direct compliment to James as the worthy successor to Queen Elizabeth. The Queen appears as a baby at the play's end.

> In her days every man shall eat in safety
> Under his own vine what he plants, and sing
> The merry songs of peace to all his neighbours . . .
> Nor shall this peace sleep with her, but, as when
> The bird of wonder dies—the maiden phoenix–
> Her ashes create another heir
> As great in admiration as herself. . .
> Who from the sacred ashes of her honour

Shall star-like rise as great in fame as she was,
And so stand fixed.
Wherever the bright sun of heaven shall shine,
His honour and the greatness of his name
Shall be, and make new nations . . . Our children's children
Shall see this, and bless heaven.

All is True, Act 5 Scene 4, lines 32–35, 39–42, 45–47, 50–52, 53–54

THE BURNING OF THE GLOBE

All is True was performed at The Globe on June 29, 1613. A merchant named Henry Bluett saw the performance. A few days later he wrote a letter about what he had seen.

> On Tuesday last there was acted at the Globe a new play called *All is True*, which had been acted not passing two or three times before. There came many people to see it insomuch that the house was very full, and as the play was almost ended the house was fired with shooting off a chamber which was stopped with tow which was blown up into the thatch of the house and so burned down to the ground. But the people escaped all without hurt except one man who was scalded with the fire by adventuring in to save a child which otherwise had been burnt.

Soon after The Globe burned down, Henslowe and Alleyn, whose Fortune playhouse had been the Bankside theater's main competitor, moved back south of the Thames River. They built a new playhouse at the Beargardens on the east side of the street, which today is still called Bear Garden, just west of the modern Southwark Bridge. The Hope was a dual-purpose building with a removable stage. This enabled the standing area to be used for animal baiting. The stench from the animals, which must have lingered when plays were performed, would have been appalling even for those days. Ben Jonson wrote a play, *Bartholomew Fair,* for the Hope playhouse in 1614. In his play, the characters gamble, cheat, eat greasy pork, and vomit prodigiously. The play was a huge, sprawling exploration of London low life. It probably summed up the qualities of this end of the popular theater market.

The Globe was almost certainly very different. The rebuilt Globe cost the **sharers** £1,400, about $2,250. When the Globe reopened for business, it held up to 3,000 people. The roof was tiled this time, rather than thatched, but the main dimensions of the stage seem to have stayed the same. It is possible that Shakespeare left the King's Men at this time and retired to Stratford for good. There is no record of any shares in the playhouse in Shakespeare's will a couple of years later. Knowing that he took the long-term view in the matter of the Stratford tithes, it seems strange that he did not hang on to a share in the Globe as an investment.

Whatever his connections were with the new Globe, it seems certain that Shakespeare was back in Stratford by September 1614. At this time he got involved in a plan by another Stratford man, William Combe, to enclose land on the Welcombe fields to the north of the town.

Enclosure was an important strategy for the new farming **gentry**. The old system of subsistence farming, in which people grew just enough to feed their own families, had parceled out land between many farmers over a wide area. Enclosure involved an agreement by the larger landowners to bring their land together into larger areas. These areas were then fenced and farmed as a unit. For the poorer farmers and laborers, this was a threat to their survival. The traditional access to the leftovers from harvesting was likely to disappear, which would remove a source of food for the winter. In addition, enclosure was often in the interest of providing more pasture for sheep. This would employ far fewer people than raising traditional crops, such as corn and barley. Enclosure threatened to cause widespread unemployment. Enclosure may also have contributed to famine as poor harvests, such as those in 1607 and 1608, were made worse because less land was being farmed.

In 1614, Shakespeare was the chief landowner in these fields. He seems to have been courted both by the town authorities, who opposed the enclosure that Combe was proposing, and by Combe himself. Interestingly, Shakespeare seems to have been struck by an attack of indecision. The evidence does point to him siding with Combe, which made the council push harder to get him to change his mind.

During the first months of 1615, there was some violence against Combe, who had been digging ditches to get the enclosure under way. But in April, the town authorities got a court order to prevent him from proceeding. Combe did not give up, but Shakespeare's involvement soon ended with his death.

In February 1616, Shakespeare's youngest daughter, Judith, then 31 years old, married Thomas Quiney. The Shakespeare and Quiney families were often intertwined in Stratford life. Richard Quiney had asked Shakespeare for a loan to help with his expenses when visiting London on **corporation** business, and the playwright had agreed to assist. Thomas Quiney was less lucky.

Judith and Thomas married without a proper church license. This immediately put them in trouble with the authorities. Then a month after they were married, Thomas was called before Stratford's bawdy court. This is a local church court overseen by the **vicar**. Thomas was found guilty of causing another woman, Margaret Wheeler, to be pregnant. She and her infant died and were buried together on March 15. Quiney was sentenced to public humiliation and a fine of 5 **shillings,** or about 40 cents, which was more than a week's wages for a laborer. One of the results of this seems to have been that the day before Quiney was brought before the court, and presumably having told his father-in-law the truth, Shakespeare altered his will, cutting Thomas out of it.

THE LAST WILL AND TESTAMENT

By the time he altered his will on March 25, William Shakespeare appears to have been dying. The signature at the bottom of every page is weak and scratchy. As a man of property and business, with a wife and adult children to take care of, his will is straightforward. While the will gives some insights into the situation he and his family found themselves in, it gives no real surprises.

To his eldest daughter Susanna and her husband Dr. John Hall, he left the houses and land he owned in Stratford, the house he had recently bought at the Blackfriars, and his other London interests. The London interests may have included shares in one or the other of the King's Men's playhouses, but there is no evidence for this. Their daughter Elizabeth was given his silver.

To his second daughter Judith, he left £100, or about $160, and promised a further £50 on condition that she give up the cottage in Chapel Lane. He also agreed to give her, or any of her children still living in 1619, a further £150, or about $240. If she remained married, she would get this as a 10 percent annual interest payment. This effectively prevented Thomas Quiney from getting his hands on her money. It also gave her some separate means of support if necessary. Judith also received Shakespeare's "broad silver and gilt bowl."

His sister Joan, the only other surviving child of John and Mary Shakespeare, was allowed to live at the Henley Street house until she died, but she had to pay rent of 1 shilling, about 8 cents, a year. Her sons William, Michael, and Thomas all received £5, or $8. Other bequests included £19, about $30, for the poor of Stratford, money to provide a memorial in Stratford church, money to a number of Stratford men to buy rings in his memory, and

> to my Fellowes John Hemminge, Richard Burbage & Henry Cundell xxvjs viijd A peece (26 shillings 8 pence each) to buy them Ringes.

It was a common practice at this time for people to enable their friends to remember them after their death by wearing memorial rings.

Almost at the end of the will, he makes a last strange, but famous, bequest.

> Item, I gyve unto my wife my second-best bed, with the furniture.

It should not be assumed that this was all that William was giving to his wife, Anne, of whom little is known about since her marriage. She would have received the standard "widow's portion" from her husband's goods and property. This varied from place to place, and it is not known exactly what it was in Stratford. It probably included the right to live at New Place until she died. The gift of "the second-best bed" was most likely a token of love and affection. The best bed in a house in Shakespeare's time would have been reserved for special guests. The second-best bed was the one in which Anne and William slept.

Within a few weeks of making these alterations to the will, Shakespeare was dead. He died on April 23, 1616, in Stratford. He was buried on April 25 in Holy Trinity Church. As befitted an important and wealthy citizen of the town, he was buried inside the church near the altar at the east end. A monument to his memory was placed on the wall near the grave. Shakespeare himself left the money to pay for the monument, which was carved by Gerard Johnson. Johnson's workshops were near The Globe theater in London.

BY ME WILLIAM SHAKESPEARE

Anne Shakespeare died at the age of 67 in 1623. William's other long-time companion, Richard Burbage, died in 1619. The opposition, in the person of Philip Henslowe, died just before Shakespeare, in January 1616.

But many of the King's Men who had known Shakespeare, long outlived him. Two in particular, John Heminges and Henry Condell, who had received

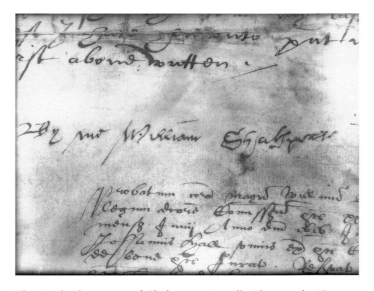

This is the last page of Shakespeare's will. The words "By me, William Shakespeare" are in his own handwriting. The will is now in the Public Records Office, London.

money for memorial rings, took it upon themselves to offer something more permanent in his name. No doubt they had a lot of help from their colleagues.

At the end of his will, Shakespeare wrote as an affirmation,

by me, William Shakespeare.

He rarely made the same affirmation for his work after the publication of *Venus and Adonis* and *The Rape of Lucrece*. The publication of plays had always been a tricky thing. Plays were the property of the players or their manager. For many years, the printing of a play meant to lose a precious asset. Once a play was publicly available, any company could use them.

In 1616, another playwright, Ben Jonson, took the bold step of collecting his stage works together and publishing them. It was a huge volume of over 1,000 pages. This says a good deal about Jonson, who believed strongly in the right of any author to have his work recognized, published and, if possible, praised. Jonson's book also created a precedent that Heminges and Condell were prepared to follow. They too collected the plays of "so excellent fellow as was our Shakespeare" and published them.

The so-called First **Folio** of Shakespeare's plays appeared in 1623. It contains almost all the plays he is known to have written. It does not include *Pericles, Prince of Tyre*, written in 1608 in collaboration with George Wilkins. Nor does it include the now lost *Cardenio*, written in collaboration with John Fletcher. Another omission is *Love's Labour's Won*, a title that appeared on a bookseller's list. It was presumably printed, but either no copies have survived or been found, or it is a play now known by a different name.

The plays in the **Folio** often have a complex relationship to the plays that were printed earlier in separate editions. Heminges and Condell, and those who helped them, would have had access to these earlier printed plays. They also had other material that was owned by the King's Men. Possibly they even had Shakespeare's own copies, notes, and revisions. It is a mistake, though, to think of the text of the First Folio as the only possible texts of the plays. Plays are living things. Many of Shakespeare's plays remained in the repertoire of the **Lord Chamberlain's** Men and the King's Men for 30 years before the Folio was put together. The plays would have grown and changed with experience and circumstance during that time.

A play text is only one part of a play. It may give indications about other things. It may tell stage directions, for instance, but much else remains a matter for the actor playing before an audience. Gesture, voice intonation, looks, where performers are on stage, costume, silences, and pauses all contribute to a play. These things are not contained in editions such as the First Folio. Above all, the plays are alive only when they are being performed. The experience of what works in front of an audience causes changes. Some of these changes seep into even the most fixed text.

It is important scholarly work to try to find a text that represents as closely as possible what Lord Strange's Men or the Lord Chamberlain's Men or the King's Men actually said. This gives clues to the intention of the performers and the playwright. It may even offer insights into how they were performed. But the plays also have a history after the First Folio. Many of the plays remained in the repertoire of the King's Men until the victorious **Puritan** faction in the country closed the playhouses in 1642. Quite a few plays returned to the stage with the reopening of theaters after King Charles II was returned to the throne in 1660. The plays were cut and rewritten to meet changes in taste. "Original" texts were rediscovered, but rarely performed in unmodified forms. They were changed again, and returned to a semblance of historical accuracy. They have been translated, criticized, read, and performed countless times around the world since 1623.

Today it is possible to see how the plays developed even during Shakespeare's lifetime. Directors can work with the whole range of possibilities from **Quartos** and Folios to help them decide how to direct the plays. Sometimes they make large changes, such as moving the order of the scenes, shifting lines from one place to another, or even writing new lines. There is nothing new in this approach. It is an essential part of the ongoing life of the theater.

The First Folio is a wonderful and indispensable monument to a great playwright and man of the theater. But like all monuments, its best use is for it to give directions. The First Folio can act as a landmark for new interactions between actors and audience. The text is a springboard for new encounters with these living plays.

YEAR	THEATER HISTORY	WILLIAM SHAKESPEARE'S LIFE AND FAMILY	IMPORTANT EVENTS AND PERSONALITIES
c700B.C.E.			Homer's *Iliad* probably reaches its final written form
c400B.C.E	Ancient Greek drama at its high point		
c200B.C.E	Plautus (c254–184) writing comedies		
43B.C.E			Ovid born (d A.D.17)
c4B.C.E	Seneca born (d A.D.65)		
410C.E.			Roman rule in Britain ends
1066			Norman conquest of Britain
1196			Stratford-upon-Avon becomes a borough
1311	First York Corpus Christi mystery plays performed		
1345	Geoffrey Chaucer born (d 1400)		
1348			During two years, the Black Death kills 25 percent of the population of Europe
1469			Niccolo Machiavelli born (d 1527)
1490			Stratford's Clopton Bridge is built
1533			Montaigne born (d 1592)
1535			English Church separates from the authority of Rome
1538	First public playhouse built in Great Yarmouth		
1552		John Shakespeare recorded working in Henley St., Stratford	
1553			Stratford granted Charter of Incorporation
1554	John Lyly born (d 1606)		
1557		John Shakespeare marries Mary Arden	
1558	Thomas Kyd born (d 1594) George Peele born (d 1597)	Joan (d 1558) born to John and Mary	Elizabeth Tudor becomes Queen of England
1560	Robert Greene born (d 1592)		
1562		Margaret (d 1563) born to John and Mary	
1564	Christopher Marlowe born (d 1593)	William born to John and Mary. Baptized April 26 John is Chamberlain of Stratford	20 percent of Stratford dies of the plague

Year		
1566	EDWARD ALLEYN BORN (D 1626)	GILBERT (D 1612) BORN TO JOHN AND MARY
1567	PUBLIC PLAYHOUSE THE RED LION OPENED IN LONDON RICHARD BURBAGE BORN (D 1619)	QUEEN ELIZABETH SEES MYSTERY PLAYS DURING VISIT TO COVENTRY
1569	THE QUEEN'S MEN VISIT STRATFORD	
1570		JOAN (2) BORN TO JOHN AND MARY, JOHN IS BAILIFF OF STRATFORD WILLIAM PROBABLY BEGINS TO ATTEND STRATFORD GRAMMAR SCHOOL
1571		ANNE (D 1579) BORN TO JOHN AND MARY
1572	STROLLING PLAYERS FORCED TO FIND PATRONS AFTER PASSAGE OF ACT PUNISHING ROGUES AND VAGABONDS BEN JONSON BORN (D 1637)	
1573	INIGO JONES BORN (D 1652) EARL OF LEICESTER'S MEN PLAY IN STRATFORD	
1574	EARL OF LEICESTER'S MEN RECEIVE ROYAL LICENSE	RICHARD (D 1613) BORN TO JOHN AND MARY
1575	ST. PAUL'S BOYS GIVE PUBLIC PERFORMANCES	QUEEN ELIZABETH SEES PLAYS AND PAGEANTS DURING VISIT TO KENILWORTH
1576	JAMES BURBAGE BUILDS THE THEATRE IN LONDON BOYS OF THE CHAPEL ROYAL PERFORM AT BLACKFRIARS	
1577	HENRY LANEMAN BUILDS THE CURTAIN THEATRE IN LONDON	RAPHAEL HOLINSHED'S *CHRONICLES* FIRST PUBLISHED
1579	JOHN FLETCHER BORN (D 1625)	
1580	LAST PERFORMANCE OF COVENTRY MYSTERY CYCLE	EDMUND (D 1607) BORN TO JOHN AND MARY
1581		WILLIAM MAY BE IN LANCASHIRE
1582		WILLIAM MARRIES ANNE HATHAWAY IN NOVEMBER
1583	NEW COMPANY OF QUEEN'S MEN PLAYERS ESTABLISHED	SUSANNA BORN TO WILLIAM AND ANNE, BAPTIZED IN MAY WILLIAM SHAKESPEARE'S CATHOLIC COUSIN ARRESTED ON WAY TO ASSASSINATE QUEEN
1584	FRANCIS BEAUMONT BORN (D 1616)	
1585		TWINS JUDITH AND HAMNET BORN TO WILLIAM AND ANNE, BAPTIZED IN JANUARY
1586		WILLIAM MAY HAVE LEFT STRATFORD FOR LONDON AROUND THIS TIME
	SIR PHILIP SIDNEY, POET, KILLED AT BATTLE OF ZUTPHEN	
	MARY QUEEN OF SCOTS IS EXECUTED	
1587	THE ROSE THEATRE BUILT IN LONDON CHRISTOPHER MARLOWE'S *DOCTOR FAUSTUS* AND *TAMBURLAINE* ARE WRITTEN WILLIAM KNELL OF THE QUEEN'S MEN KILLED AT THAME	

YEAR	THEATER HISTORY	WILLIAM SHAKESPEARE'S LIFE AND FAMILY	THE WORKS OF WILLIAM SHAKESPEARE (MOST DATES ARE APPROXIMATE)	IMPORTANT EVENTS AND PERSONALITIES
1588				THE SPANISH ARMADA IS DESTROYED
1589	MARLOWE'S *JEW OF MALTA* WRITTEN			
1591	PEELE'S *THE OLD WIVES' TALE* WRITTEN		*TWO GENTLEMEN OF VERONA* WRITTEN	
1592	PLAGUE CLOSES PLAYHOUSES BEGINNING IN JUNE	WILLIAM ATTACKED BY ROBERT GREENE AS "AN UPSTART CROW"	*THE FIRST PART OF THE CONTENTION. . . THE TRUE TRAGEDY OF RICHARD, DUKE OF YORK* WRITTEN *HENRY VI PART I* PERFORMED IN MARCH	
1593	PLAYHOUSES STILL CLOSED MARLOWE KILLED		*RICHARD III* FIRST PERFORMED (OUTSIDE LONDON) *VENUS AND ADONIS* PRINTED *LOVE'S LABOUR'S LOST* WRITTEN	
1594	THE QUEEN'S MEN DISBANDED	WILLIAM JOINS THE LORD CHAMBERLAIN'S MEN	*THE TAMING OF THE SHREW*, *TITUS ANDRONICUS*, AND *THE RAPE OF LUCRECE* PRINTED, *COMEDY OF ERRORS* PERFORMED DECEMBER 28	
1595	THE SWAN THEATRE BUILT IN LONDON BY FRANCIS LANGLEY		*ROMEO AND JULIET*, *A MIDSUMMER NIGHT'S DREAM*, AND *RICHARD II* WRITTEN	
1596	JAMES BURBAGE LEASES BLACKFRIARS BUILDINGS	WILLIAM AND ANNE'S SON, HAMNET, DIES JOHN SHAKESPEARE GRANTED COAT-OF-ARMS	*KING JOHN*, *THE MERCHANT OF VENICE*, AND *HENRY IV PART I* WRITTEN	
1597	JAMES BURBAGE DIES	WILLIAM BUYS NEW PLACE, STRATFORD	*THE MERRY WIVES OF WINDSOR* AND *HENRY IV PART II* WRITTEN	
1598	THE THEATRE DEMOLISHED JONSON'S *EVERY MAN* WRITTEN		*MUCH ADO ABOUT NOTHING* WRITTEN	GEORGE CHAPMAN'S (1559–1636) ENGLISH TRANSLATIONS OF HOMER'S *ILIAD* PUBLISHED
1599	THE (FIRST) GLOBE THEATRE BUILT		*HENRY V* AND *JULIUS CAESAR* WRITTEN	
1600	THE FORTUNE THEATRE BUILT		*AS YOU LIKE IT* WRITTEN FIRST VERSION OF *HAMLET* WRITTEN	
1601		JOHN SHAKESPEARE DIES	*TWELFTH NIGHT* WRITTEN	
1602			*TROILUS AND CRESSIDA* WRITTEN	

Year				
1603	PLAGUE CLOSES LONDON THEATERS BEGINNING IN MAY	WILLIAM'S COMPANY OF PLAYERS RECEIVE ROYAL AUTHORITY ON MAY 19		QUEEN ELIZABETH I DIES / CORONATION OF KING JAMES I JULY 25
1604	LONDON THEATERS REOPEN IN APRIL		*TIMON OF ATHENS* WRITTEN / *OTHELLO* PERFORMED NOVEMBER 1 / *MEASURE FOR MEASURE* PERFORMED DECEMBER 26	CORONATION PROCESSION OF JAMES I, MARCH 15
1605	THE ROSE THEATRE PROBABLY DEMOLISHED		*ALL'S WELL THAT ENDS WELL*	THE GUNPOWDER PLOT FAILS ON NOVEMBER 5
1606			*MACBETH* AND *ANTONY AND CLEOPATRA* WRITTEN	
1607		WILLIAM AND ANNE'S DAUGHTER, SUSANNA, MARRIES DR. JOHN HALL / WILLIAM'S BROTHER, EDMUND, DIES IN DECEMBER	*PERICLES, PRINCE OF TYRE* WRITTEN	
1608	KING'S MEN MOVE INTO BLACKFRIARS THEATRE	WILLIAM'S GRANDDAUGHTER, ELIZABETH, BORN / WILLIAM'S MOTHER, MARY, DIES	FIRST VERSION OF *KING LEAR* PRINTED / *CORIOLANUS* WRITTEN	
1609			*SONNETS* AND *A LOVER'S COMPLAINT* PRINTED	
1611			*THE WINTER'S TALE*, *CYMBELINE*, AND *THE TEMPEST* PERFORMED	
1612				HENRY, ELDEST SON OF KING JAMES I, DIES
1613	THE FIRST GLOBE THEATRE BURNS DOWN IN JUNE DURING A PERFORMANCE OF *ALL IS TRUE*		*ALL IS TRUE* AND *TWO NOBLE KINSMEN*	ACTOR-THEATER OWNER EDWARD ALLEYN FOUNDS DULWICH COLLEGE IN LONDON. / KING JAMES DAUGHTER, ELIZABETH, MARRIES
1614	THE SECOND GLOBE THEATRE BUILT / THE HOPE THEATRE BUILT			
1616	PHILIP HENSLOWE DIES	WILLIAM DIES IN APRIL, POSSIBLY ON APRIL 23 / WILLIAM AND ANNE'S DAUGHTER, JUDITH, MARRIES THOMAS QUINEY		
1619	RICHARD BURBAGE DIES			
1621	THE FORTUNE THEATRE BURNS DOWN			
1623		ANNE SHAKESPEARE DIES	THE FIRST FOLIO PUBLISHED	

KEY

Playhouses

1. The Theatre (1576–1598)
2. The Curtain (1577–?1627)
3. The Fortune (1600–1621, rebuilt 1623–1662, unused after 1649)
4. The Red Lion (mentioned in 1567)
5. Cross Keys Inn (in use for some years from at least 1579)
6. The Rose (?1587–?1605)
7. The Globe (1599–1613, rebuilt 1614–1644)
8. The Swan (1595–?1637)
9. The Hope (1614–1656, unused after 1642)

Other locations

10. Church of St Mary, Overy
11. The Bear Garden
12. St Olave's Parish
13. The Middle Temple
14. Carter Lane
15. Ireland's Yard
16. Shoreditch High Street
17. Holywell Lane
18. Gracechurch Street
19. Bishopsgate
20. Poultry
21. Cheapside
22. Eastcheap
23. Fenchurch Street
24. St Paul's Churchyard
25. Liberty of the Manor of Paris Gardens
26. Liberty of the Clink
27. Liberty of Finsbury
28. Whitecross Street
29. St Helen's Parish
30. Silver Street
31. The Blackfriars

Shakespeare's London

To Whitehall

St Paul's

River Thames

0   1 km

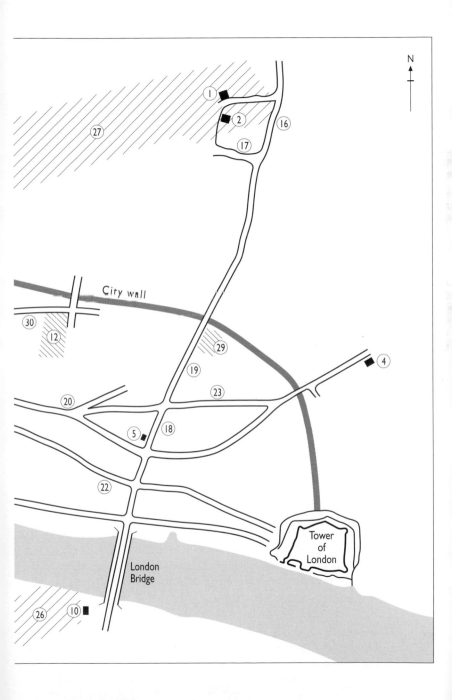

NOTES FOR FURTHER STUDY

Quotations throughout this book are from the single-volume critical edition edited by Stanley Wells and Gary Taylor: *William Shakespeare: The Complete Works*, Oxford University Press, 1986. There are many other editions of individual plays and poems. The Arden, New Arden series, and the New Penguin Shakespeare are clear and have good critical introductions and notes. The Penguin Critical Studies series is more advanced, but fascinating. The following are also recommended.

Ashby, Ruth. *Elizabethan England*. Tarrytown, NY: Marshall Cavendish, 1998.

Bate, Jonathan. *The Genius of Shakespeare*. London: Macmillan/Picador, 1997.

Claybourne, Anna and Rebecca Treays. *World of Shakespeare*. Tulsa, OK: E D C Publishing. 1997.

Cox, John D. and David Scott Kaplan, eds. *A New History of Early English Drama*. New York: Columbia University Press, 1997.

Greenblatt, Stephen. *Shakespearean Negotiations*. Oxford University Press, 1990.

Gurr, Andrew. *The Shakespearean Stage, 1574–1642*. Cambridge: Cambridge University Press, 1980.
——. *Playgoing in Shakespeare's London*. Cambridge: Cambridge University Press, 1996.

Honan, Park. *Shakespeare: A Life*. Oxford: Clarendon Press, 1998.

Laroque François. *Shakespeare: Court, Crowd, and Playhouse*. London: Thames and Hudson, New Horizons, 1993.

Michaels, Wendy. *Playbuilding Shakespeare*. New York: Cambridge University Press, 1997.

Morley, Jacqueline. *Shakespeare's Theater*. Lincolnwood, Ill: NTC Contemporary Publishing Company, 1994.

Schoenbaum, S. *William Shakespeare: A Compact Documentary Life*. Oxford: Oxford University Press, 1986.

Thomson, Peter *Shakespeare's Professional Career*. Cambridge: Cambridge University Press, 1992.

Additional Resources

African-American Shakespeare Company
5214-F Diamond Heights Blvd.
PMB 923
San Francisco, CA 94131
Tel: (415) 333-1918
This company's mission is to produce European classical works
with an African-American cultural perspective

Royal Shakespeare Company
Waterside
Stratford-Upon-Avon
Warwickshire CV37 6BB
Tel: 011 441789 296655
Royal Shakespeare Company can provide details of performances
of plays and background information, as well as education packs.

Shakespeare Birthplace Trust
Henley Street
Stratford-upon-Avon
Warwickshire CV37 6QW
Tel: 011 441789 204016
This organization maintains the Shakespeare Centre Library,
holding details of local history and Shakespeare properties in
Stratford.

The Shakespeare Theatre
516 8th Street SE
Washington, DC 20003
(202) 547-3230
One of the top Shakespeare companies in the U.S., its mission is
to produce and preserve classical theater and to develop new
audiences for classical theater.

Glossary

alderman senior elected member of a town or city council

apprentice young person being trained in a trade

bailiff senior elected member of the borough council, the equivalent of today's mayor

bearbaiting sport in which dogs fight a chained bear

bergamasque country dance, originally associated with the town of Bergamo in Italy

borough town whose local government is organized by royal charter that gives the town special privileges

boy players professional child actors, usually linked with the Chapel Royal or St. Paul's Cathedral

brothel house of prostitution

bullbaiting sport of tormenting bulls by dogs

burgess citizen of a **borough**. The burgess often has special responsibilities in the town.

Catholic a term used after the Reformation to describe those who held allegiance to the Pope

Chamberlain officer appointed by the town council to take care of the borough's financial affairs

chorus in ancient Greek drama, a group of performers who observe, comment on, and sometimes participate in the action of the play

cockfighting sport in which roosters fight

commedia (*commedia dell'arte*) highly improvised, energetic comedy, developed in Italy in the 1400s and 1500s

corporation town whose rules of government place responsibility on a group of elected members to act together

Corpus Christi Catholic church festival established in 1311 celebrating the Body and Blood of Christ

dramatic irony key dramatic effect and situation; moments in a play when the audience is aware of something of which a character is not aware

farce highly physical comedy, depending on improbabilities, embarrassments, disguises, and coincidences

folio book of large page size—the edition of Shakespeare's plays put together by fellow actors after his death and published in his memory in 1623 is known as the First Folio

gentry class of people just below the nobility who gained increasing economic, social, and political power in the 1500s and 1600s in England

grammar school originally a school founded for teaching the elements of grammar, especially Latin grammar

guild term for a collection of masters of a specific skill, trade, or craft, such as The Guild of Carpenters; or the Guild of the Holy Cross was Stratford's governing body from about 1285 until 1547

guiser person in disguise as part of a popular entertainment

Jacobean just as "Elizabethan" refers to the time of Queen Elizabeth—"Jacobean" refers to King James I and his times

Jesuit member of the Roman Catholic religious order founded by Ignatius Loyola in 1534

jig bawdy dance that often ended performances of plays in Shakespeare's time

Knight of the Garter member of an order of noblemen

Liberty area just outside London where city authorities had little power; Brothels and playhouses were located there

Lord Chamberlain royal official responsible for providing entertainment at court and ensuring that plays contained nothing that would offend the ruler

Lord of Misrule term for the person appointed as mock-ruler of the feasting and entertainment during the Christmas period

Master of the Revels in Elizabethan and Jacobean times, the official in the Lord Chamberlain's office who has special responsibility for court entertainment and the control of players

mummers popular entertainers who traveled from house to house, often in disguise

mystery cycle collections of plays performed at the festival of Corpus Christi

oratory art of speaking to an audience, usually political contexts

pageant performance, on a movable stage or wagon, often of a spectacular nature

patron in Shakespeare's time, a nobleman who supported, often financially the work of poets, artists, musicians, or playing companies, often in return for flattery

plague bubonic plague is a highly infectious disease transmitted by fleas that live on rats

progress journey by a monarch through her or his lands, through which the nobility ensured that the ruler saw, and was seen by, the people in order to establish and reinforce his or her royal power

Protestant Christian who rejects the doctrines of the Roman Catholic Church and the authority of the Pope

Puritans Protestants who felt that personal responsibility and moral purity were essential to the Christian life

quarto book of smaller page size than a folio

recusant Catholic sympathizer who refused to attend the church services of the Church of England at a time when nonattendance was a crime punished by a fine

Reformation religious revolution in the 1500s that rejected key Roman Catholic doctrines, and the authority of the Pope

rhetoric art of careful and persuasive speaking and the rules for such speech

sharer player with a formal link to a playing company that allowed him to receive a percentage of the profits from performances

shilling coin worth one-twentieth of a pound sterling, or about 8 cents in value

tiring house part of the playhouse behind the stage where players could wait for their entrances, change costumes, collect extra items they might need on stage, and where scenery was probably stored

tragedy form of play that shows the downfall of a hero and the suffering and death that the downfall creates

tragicomedy form of play with elements of both tragedy and comedy, often intended to show the complexity of life

Tudor of or having to do with the time of the Tudors, who were the reigning family of England from 1485 to 1603

vicar parish minister of the Church of England who is paid a salary

INDEX

ADA
Lovelace

Lovelace

Ben Jeapes

Illustrations by Nick Ward

Abrams Books for Young Readers

NEW YORK

Library of Congress Control Number 2019950354

ISBN 978-1-4197-4075-6

Text copyright © 2020 Ben Jeapes
Illustrations copyright © 2020 Nick Ward
Book design by Charice Silverman

2019 © as U.K. edition. First published in 2019
by David Fickling Books Limited

ABRAMS The Art of Books
195 Broadway, New York, NY 10007
abramsbooks.com

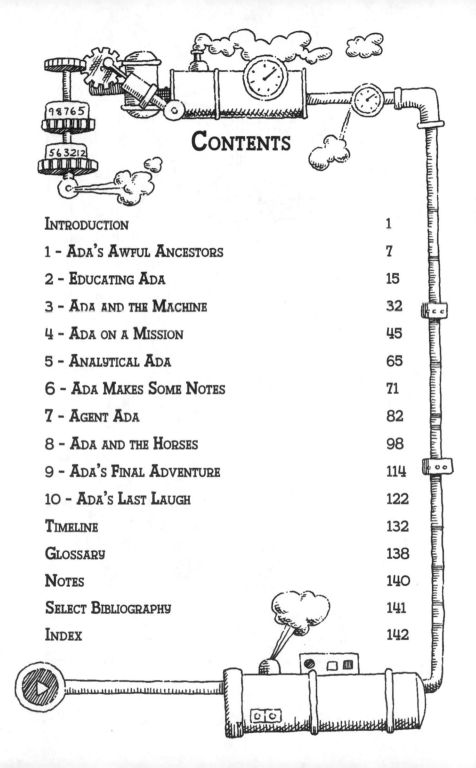

CONTENTS

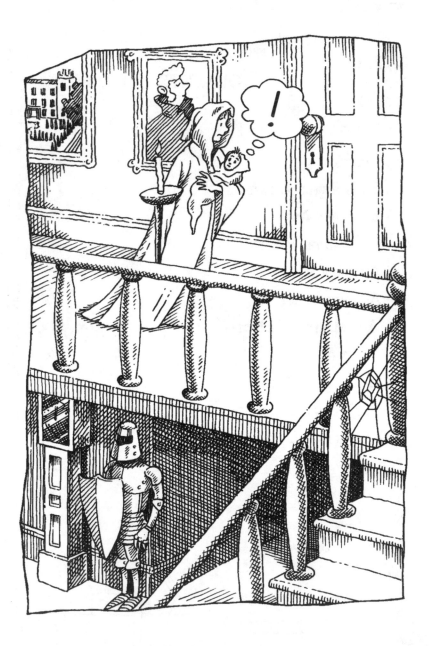

INTRODUCTION

13 Piccadilly Terrace, London, January 15, 1816

It was a freezing cold January night when **a one-month-old baby was being stolen** from her father. A woman took the baby from the nursery.

It was the wrong century for electricity and central heating. The bedrooms of the five-floor mansion were snug and warm with coal fires, but the stairs and hallways were as dark and cold as the night outside. The thief crept away with her precious bundle, terrified of being discovered. In a house this size, it was a long way from the nursery to the front door—a lot of wooden floors and stairs, ready to creak a warning.

The stairs bent under every step the woman took. She held her breath each time she put a foot down, feeling the wood flex under her weight. But no sound came.

Silver moonlight splashed across the tiles of the front hall. There was one more challenge—the big, heavy front door, bolted shut against the night. She drew the bolts back one by one and **the metallic *clunks* echoed around the house**.

One, *clunk*.

It was like an explosion in her ears. She made herself keep going. If people woke up, they would be pouring down the stairs any minute now.

Two, *clunk*.

The woman grasped the door handle and pulled.

Cre-e-e-a-a-a-k . . .

Heart pounding, she stepped out into the night.

The streets were cold, dark and misty, but the city was already stirring, getting ready for the next day. It was very unusual for an upper-class lady to be out alone at this hour. **If she wasn't careful, she would attract attention.**

There was a carriage and a driver waiting for her. The woman hurried over and the driver helped her up. Once the door closed, she felt safer. He flicked the reins and the carriage lurched off.

The woman didn't relax until she reached her destination, a hundred miles away from London. But at least her plan worked. **She had successfully stolen her daughter** from her own home. The servants in the house would have obeyed her husband, the baby's father, and prevented her escape. A man's word was law, after all, and she knew they weren't completely safe.

In 1816, machines still ran on wind, steam, clockworks, or muscle power. Only a few scientists vaguely knew about electricity, and a "computer" was a person paid to do complicated sums—or computations—on paper.

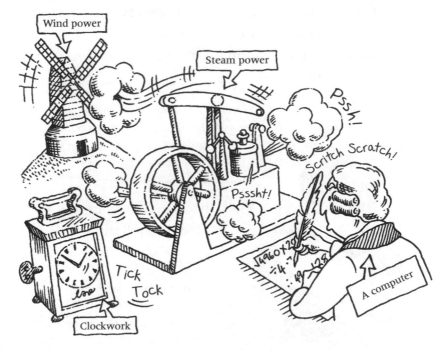

This was the world the baby in the carriage was born into. Back then, machines were designed by men. Women in the nineteenth century had hardly any education and even less power. None of those male inventors would ever have imagined that, one day, one small machine might let you count and write, watch a movie, talk to friends, and more. But when the baby grew up, she wouldn't have been surprised at all.

One day, she would have a computer software language named after her, as well as a medal for people who have made great advances in the world of computers. **There's even a day named in her honor**, to celebrate women's achievements in science, technology, engineering, and math.

All in good time, though. At that moment, she was still only a month old!

Excuse me. Ada here. I'm the baby being stolen. The "thief" is my mother, Lady Annabella Byron, and she is not a common criminal!

Well, this was how your mother liked to tell the story . . .

Yes, but she believed she was saving me from my dreadful father, who gave an altogether different account of the event.

Hmm, your mom and dad were quite, erm, **interesting**, weren't they? Maybe we should start by talking about them . . . ?

Oh, my wretched family! Very well. Start a new chapter and tell everyone about them. But brace yourselves. It won't be pretty.

Byron Family Tree

William Byron
4th Lord Byron
Surprisingly little scandal

Murderer!

William Byron
5th Lord Byron
a.k.a. "The Wicked Lord"
Killed his cousin in an argument about grouse shooting. Spent all his money, so his son wouldn't inherit it.

Vice-Admiral John Byron
a.k.a. "Foul-Weather Jack"
Naval officer and adventurer. Almost started a war by claiming possession of the Falkland Islands, which the Spanish said belonged to them.

Oops!

You rascal!

William Byron MP
Racked up gambling debts and expected his dad to pay them. Ditched a rich bride to run off with his cousin. Then died before his dad, so the Byron title went to his cousin George.

Captain John Byron Gordon
a.k.a. "Mad Jack"
Blew all his money on wild living. Married two rich women and spent all their money. Had to take a new surname (Gordon) in one marriage deal. Left £22,000 debt ($44 million today) to his son George.

Just lend me a few thousand, Dad!

Lovely cash!

George Gordon Byron
6th Lord Byron
Violent temper. Abused drugs and alcohol. Debts forced him into marriage with a rich woman. Unfaithful husband (had girlfriends and boyfriends while he was married). World-famous poet.

Poetry is such agony.

And I'm the only woman! The men had wives and mothers, but only they could be this awful, because they were in charge!

Ada Byron

1   ADA'S AWFUL ANCESTORS

Ada's father, George Gordon, was the sixth Lord Byron (let's just call him Byron for short). He came from a long line of **drunkards, addicts, gamblers, and murderers**.

He carried on the family theme of wild, dangerous living, even though he didn't have any money before he got married! He liked to throw parties for his friends at the family home, Newstead Abbey in Nottinghamshire. Newstead had once been a monastery, and it's said Byron liked to drink his wine out of a cup made from an old skull found in the monks' graveyard. Ew! Byron started writing poetry at the age of fourteen, and in 1812, when he was twenty-four, he published the first half of his epic poem, *Childe Harold's Pilgrimage*—it sold out in just three days! **Byron became a superstar overnight.** In those days, he was about as cool as a YouTuber with fifty million followers. As he said himself: *I awoke one morning and found myself famous.*

Just think what he could have done if he'd written the whole poem!

Childe Harold made a small fortune for its publisher, but it didn't help Byron's debt problems. Strangely, he **wouldn't take any of the money** for himself.

My father loved being difficult. He believed only common people got paid, and he didn't want anyone to think he was common. I used to think the same thing, until I realized money is actually quite useful.

Byron's money troubles finally changed when he met Anne Isabella Milbanke.

HORRENDOUS HONEYMOON

Anne Isabella called herself Annabella. She was the cousin of a future prime minister and stood to inherit £20,000 (a few million dollars today) from a very old uncle. For Byron, it was the money that sealed the deal. In those days every penny a woman owned officially became her husband's when they got married— and then she had **absolutely no control over it**.

Byron might not want to earn money, but he had no problem with marrying a rich woman and taking all her wealth. It was a family tradition after all!

There was more to the match than just money,
however. Byron and Annabella agreed about
important things like social justice and helping people
who were too poor to help themselves. His first speech
in the House of Lords had been about workers in the
north of England losing their jobs because of new
fangled machines taking their places. **Byron was on
the workers' side and so was Annabella.**

THE HOUSE OF LORDS

Britain's Parliament consists of the House of Commons and
the House of Lords. Members of the Commons are elected, but
to join the Lords, you just needed to *be* a lord. So, Byron was
automatically a member. He did have to give a speech, though,
and a member's first speech was usually on a subject very close
to their heart.

They got married on January 2, 1815, had their
first big argument on their honeymoon—it was
downhill from then on. The unhappy couple moved
to a fashionable part of London, and ten months later,

on December 10, 1815, Ada was born. She was christened Augusta Ada Gordon, but generally addressed as Miss Byron. And to avoid confusion with her father's half-sister—also named Augusta—she was known by family and friends as Ada.

Byron cared about Ada—he even wrote a bit about her in the second part of *Childe Harold*, and by his standards that's probably the nicest thing he could have done.

But he wasn't ready to be tied down, and other things were going wrong too. Annabella's uncle had finally died, but then Byron learned, to his horror, that the old man's money would go to Annabella's mother first. **Byron wouldn't get a penny until she died.** By now Byron owed so much that debt collectors moved into his London home to make sure he didn't run off with any of the valuables.

The pressure of their money troubles made Byron so **angry and violent** that his personal servant had to be on constant guard to make sure he didn't attack his wife. Meanwhile, Annabella was worried that Byron was going mad—and she wasn't too pleased to discover that, despite being married, he was still having other relationships.

By January 15, 1816, Annabella had had enough. She was worried about her money and her own safety—and if she wasn't safe, then neither was her baby. That's why she ended up sneaking away from Byron, taking Ada with her.

MEANWHILE, BACK ON THE CARRIAGE . . .

Rattling as fast as it could toward Kirkby Hall, near Leicester—where Annabella's parents lived—the journey lasted days. Byron might have guessed where his wife was heading, but with no money, he couldn't afford to chase after her. However, the law was still on his side. If she was caught, she'd have to hand Ada back. So, when they stopped overnight to rest the horses, Annabella barely slept.

It was practically unheard of for a wife to leave her husband back then. **Annabella's reputation was at risk!** Even though Byron was a horrible husband, everyone would say *she* was the one in the wrong.

She wrote to a helpful doctor, who she hoped could prove Byron was mad. If he was mad, she reckoned, then he could be cured, and they could all get back to being one fairly unhappy family.

When they reached Kirkby Hall, Annabella could finally relax . . . a little. Her rich dad, Sir Ralph Milbanke, was there to protect her, while her anxious mom hurried off to London to find the best lawyer she could.

When Annabella got the doctor's report, it said there was nothing wrong with Byron: he wasn't mad, he was just bad. There was no hope for their marriage now, because **Byron would never change**.

By that time, however, Annabella had found herself a way out of the relationship that would protect her own reputation. One of Byron's old girlfriends had revealed a secret about Byron SO SCANDALOUS, that we can't even tell you what it was. Annabella threatened to spread the secret around unless Byron stayed away.

He didn't argue.

12

AND WHAT ABOUT ADA?

Baby Ada enjoyed living with her grandparents. It was nice being with grown-ups who didn't argue all the time. She ate, she slept, she grew . . . Then, in April 1816, when Ada was three months old, Annabella received the best possible news. **Byron had fled to Europe!** In those days, if you owed money, you could be sent to jail, even if you were a lord. Too many people in England wanted Byron arrested, so he'd quickly made plans to leave the country.

And he'd fled in style. Somehow persuading the bailiffs to look the other way, Byron had sold off just about everything he owned, for whatever he could get. He'd written to Annabella, enclosing a ring for Ada, and then he'd traveled to Dover in a fancy carriage just like one the French Emperor Napoleon owned. It would have cost $600,000 today—if Byron had actually paid for it, which of course he hadn't!

2   EDUCATING ADA

Little Ada quickly settled into life at Kirkby Hall. It was a big, exciting house and she loved to toddle around its huge rooms and corridors and galleries.

She had no idea that her grandmother slept with loaded pistols by her bed, or that burly servants patrolled the grounds to **fight off any potential kidnappers**. Byron might be gone, but the law was still on his side; he could change his mind and come home one day to reclaim Ada.

So Ada didn't get out much. But it wasn't just because of security. Privacy mattered too. Ada was a celebrity baby. Since her famous parents had separated, everyone wanted a glimpse of her.

Then, when Ada was eight, **Byron died** in Greece.

Being a celebrity, his death made headlines around the world. Everyone remembered where they were when they'd heard the news. Even people who had never met Byron were beside themselves. When his body was brought back to England for the funeral, the streets were lined with mourners.

Ada cried about his death when she was told, but she wasn't sure why. Annabella assumed that since Ada couldn't possibly remember her father, she must be upset because her mother was now a widow. Ada must be crying for her.

Ada might have cried more if she had realized what her father's death meant for her own childhood.

The good thing was that money stopped being a problem. With her husband dead, Annabella could take care of her own cash again and spend it very, *very* carefully. She owned properties in London and around the country, which made her extremely rich.

And Annabella could now bring Ada up exactly how she wanted, which wasn't great for Ada. Even while Byron was abroad, Annabella had been forced to educate Ada however he had wanted. Not anymore. Now Annabella's greatest priority was to make sure Ada **didn't take after her dad**—in any way.

So Annabella **banned poetry** from the house. There were no fairy tales or bedtime stories either. Nothing to inspire the imagination. If something wasn't absolutely true, then Ada didn't need to know about it.

No Friends

Ada grew up a lonely girl. Annabella didn't let her play with the village children because they might tell her stories and spark her imagination! In any case, as far as Annabella could see, children were just small adults, so she decided Ada could hang out with carefully chosen grown-ups instead—serious, unpoetic ones.

Upper-class girls like Ada didn't go to school—school came to them! Annabella hired a whole range of tutors in "suitable" subjects: Latin, chemistry, French, music (Ada loved playing the harp), math, and shorthand (a system of symbols that make it possible to write really quickly). Ada was expected to take notes on everything she read, and because she read so much, shorthand was a speedy way of getting it all down.

To make sure Ada concentrated on her schoolwork —and didn't sneak off to write poetry instead— Annabella invented a ticket system. If Ada did well, she got tickets that she could use to buy things Annabella approved of, like books (as long as she chose the right ones).

If Ada did badly, tickets were taken away. If she was careless with her math problems, or didn't pay attention in lessons, there was a two-ticket fine. Then, if Ada ran out of tickets, **she had to stay in a cupboard** until Annabella thought she seemed ready to work again.

In the nineteenth-century, young ladies were also expected to be able to walk and stand in exactly the right way. These were important skills for attracting a future husband. Annabella worried that Ada wasn't doing it right. So, from the tender age of five, Ada had to **lie on a drawing board** for hours on end.

It was very uncomfortable and distracting.

AND WHAT ABOUT DAD?

A few weeks after Byron's body was brought back to England and buried, Annabella took Ada to visit the ship that had carried him home. To Ada it just seemed like a big, empty boat. She didn't even know what her father had looked like. How could she? There were no computers, no cameras.

Strangely, there actually was a **portrait of Byron** hanging in the house, though Annabella had hidden it behind a green curtain. She worried her daughter would react badly if she saw it.

Ada did ask to look at it, when she was little . . .

Noooo! Not even a peek until you are married, young lady!

Are you surprised that I learned to be a little afraid of my mother?

She didn't ask again.

IMAGINATION ALERT!

In 1826, when Ada was ten, her mom took her on a year-long vacation to Europe. They traveled around Switzerland and Germany and Italy, as rich people often did in those days.

Of course, there was a risk that the vacation might spark Ada's imagination, but Annabella thought it a risk worth taking. In any case, she would be with Ada every step of the way. What could possibly go wrong?

Annabella may have forgotten that in 1816, soon after he fled England, Byron had stayed in Switzerland. He'd thrown a house party on the shores of Lake Geneva for a bunch of writer friends and they'd organized a mini-competition to see who could write the best horror story. The winning story was written by an eighteen-year-old named Mary Shelley—it was called *Frankenstein*.

If there was something in the Swiss air that encouraged writers, it certainly got to Ada, because when they got home, she started writing stories too.

Once upon a time, a princess and two ladies were on vacation in the mountains . . .

None of Ada's stories would become as famous as *Frankenstein*, but it was clear **she did have an imagination**, and one day it would make her one of the most famous women of her time—but for a completely different reason.

Naturally, Annabella was not pleased that her daughter was showing signs of being creative. Something had to be done!

MATH, MORALS, AND MINDS

Annabella had her devoted doctor, Dr. King, examine Ada. He came up with a theory that Ada had "moral incontinence."

Incontinence usually means that you can't control going to the bathroom. But "*moral* incontinence," according to Dr. King, meant that Ada couldn't control her wild, random thoughts or her imagination.

There was a cure, Ada's mom was relieved to hear: it was math! **Lots and lots of math**. So, while other children learned "Twinkle, Twinkle Little Star," Ada had to memorize complicated mathematical equations.

In those days, it was quite fashionable for women to take an interest in math—up to a point. It seemed obvious to male mathematicians that women would never be able to work stuff out for themselves. Some people believed that because men's bodies were usually stronger than women's, they must have stronger minds too. So if a woman over-exercised her mind, the consequences could be disastrous!

Ada proved those mathematical men completely wrong. **She absolutely loved learning**—and she was very good at it. By the time she was twelve, she had knowledge and ideas way beyond most other twelve-year-olds, then or now. Ada believed Annabella's warnings about ending up like her father, and she desperately wanted to be sane and normal, so she threw herself into mathematics to prevent "moral incontinence," but also because:

I was desperate to know all sorts of things! Why is a rainbow always curved? Why don't planets fly off into space? And to find those answers, I needed to know math.

Annabella never realized that to be really good at math, you need a *really good* imagination. Writers and poets use words to tell stories. To Ada, mathematical symbols were like a language, which could tell a different sort of story. Putting math and imagination together she came up with an amazing idea . . .

ADA SPREADS HER WINGS

Crunch. Snap. Squelch.

And other disgusting noises that you really don't want to hear coming from under your bed. Especially when you're lying on it.

Ada was twelve years old and her cat, Puff, was eating a bird. She laid there for a while and listened to the sounds of crunching bones. Poor bird. She pictured the beautiful creature—alive—in her mind's eye. Sleek and feathered, it was perfectly designed for flight. (She tried not to think about what was happening under her bed.)

$$\text{Lift} = C^L \times (\tfrac{1}{2}\rho V^2) \times A$$
$$\text{Drag} = C^D \times (\tfrac{1}{2}\rho V^2) \times A$$

SQUELCH!
CRUNCH!

Hmm. A human can flap their arms up and down and they'll just get tired arms. A bird gives a wave of its wings and up it goes.

The year was 1828, and by then scientists knew roughly how wings worked. They just didn't know how to make a machine that would move fast enough for the air to lift it off the ground. They did know that getting off the ground needed quite complicated math. Get that right, and **anyone could fly**. Even Ada. In theory.

Ada found herself carried away by the idea. She started to study the bodies of dead birds, especially their wings, to work out how they did it.

She studied their bones and muscles too, trying to understand how the whole body of a bird helps it fly.

She decided to call her new science of how to fly . . . "flyology" and she planned to write a book about it!

FLYOLOGY, BY MISS A. BYRON, AGE 12½

And humans think they're so clever . . .

The size of a bird's wings depends on the size and weight of bird. Human wings would need to be big . . . but not too big.

These wings are too heavy—won't fly.

These wings are too small—won't fly.

These wings are just the right size!

Made of silk (lightweight but tough)

Waterproofed with oil

Stiffened with wire

Ada **tricked out a room with ropes and pulleys**, to help practice moving through the air. She drew up plans for a flying machine that could be used to deliver mail. That way, the mailman could travel in straight lines (much faster) and avoid annoying obstacles like mountains and rivers that slowed him down.

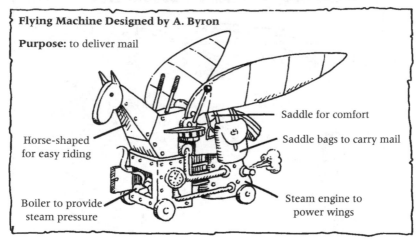

Flying Machine Designed by A. Byron

Purpose: to deliver mail

Horse-shaped for easy riding

Saddle for comfort

Saddle bags to carry mail

Boiler to provide steam pressure

Steam engine to power wings

MEASLES. PHEW!

Flyology was Ada's first real attempt to combine science and imagination, and it kept her busy for most of 1828. She also kept up her normal studies and started to work on a planetarium—a map of the night sky—showing the nearest planets to Earth and a lot of the major stars.

Then in 1829, when Ada was thirteen, **she fell ill**. She'd been getting terrible headaches since the age of seven. Now she had a really bad case of measles.

Today, measles can be prevented by a simple vaccination, but that wasn't available in the nineteenth century. Measles was much more common then, and it was often deadly. Ada's measles kept her practically paralyzed and **in bed for the next three years**! At sixteen, she was still walking with crutches, and she was plagued with aches, pains, and "nervous attacks" for the rest of her life.

Who knows, if she'd kept at flyology, Ada might have made a discovery that could have made flight work. But by the time she was better, she'd realized that the right technology just didn't exist yet. She stopped working on her flyology book and stopped writing stories, and as she started getting better, her mom breathed a sigh of relief.

ARGUING ADA

Meanwhile, the relationship between mother and daughter was still a stormy one, especially since Annabella had brought in some friends—three unmarried women—to keep an eye on Ada. **Ada nicknamed them "the Furies,"** because in Greek mythology, the Furies are spiteful goddesses of vengeance. (Ada *was* allowed to read Greek myths, because they were considered essential for a good education in those days.)

The name was a perfect fit for Ada's real-life Furies, who hated her about as much as she hated them. They would exaggerate stories about Ada, to get her into trouble. Annabella always believed the Furies and **never listened to Ada's version of events**.

Ada was really starting to get on her mother's nerves. Sometimes she refused to sleep in her bed (especially once she was over the measles) or fussed about her food. Annabella complained that she turned every disagreement into "a French Revolution." And often, Ada argued with her mom *by letter*—even though they lived in the same house! (Of course, she couldn't argue by text, like today's teenagers—and she had no idea that the work she would later become famous for would help make texting possible.)

Ada's letters were always very long and very logical, so Annabella only had herself to blame. She had wanted Ada to be logical after all. And, as she got older, Ada was certainly unusual, but she wasn't mad. She wasn't poetic. **She wasn't like Byron**. Success!

Great Britain in the early nineteenth century was a very difficult place *not* to be imaginative in. Amazing things were happening.

We have factories driven by a new wonder power source called steam!

CLACK! CLATTER! CLACK! PSSst!

Steam power meant people can travel a hundred miles in just a few hours. When my father was alive it could take days by horse and carriage.

They built a National Gallery of Practical Science in London to show off all the new inventions as they came out.

Gas mask

Pocket thermometer

I'm so looking forward to visiting. It seems there is something new nearly every week.

ALL CHANGE!

People were better informed than ever about all sorts of things. The London Zoo had opened, so for the first time ever, ordinary people could see some of **the most amazing animals in the world**—zebras, kangaroos, emus, elephants, and giraffes—with their own eyes.

Why does that horse have such a long neck?

In the mid-1800s, for the first time, more people lived in cities than in the countryside—which brought new problems of poverty and hygiene. The government was just starting to take this seriously, with new laws.

In short, Ada was living in a country that was changing, and she saw that change could be a good thing. It wasn't something to be afraid of. Technology, she realized, could be helpful in every area of life.

And Ada was changing too, from a child to an adult. For a young lady of Ada's status, the most important thing was to carry on the family name—by **finding a spouse and having children**.

"The Season" was the name for a series of parties and events for people of the right social class. It was designed to make finding a husband or wife much easier. For a young woman, it began when she was presented to the king and queen.

Not all young ladies were eligible. They had to be of good character and nominated by someone who had been presented themselves (as Annabella had been, years before). After the presentation, they were officially grown-up and on the marriage market.

Yes, sooner or later, no matter how much she loved equations and inventing flying machines . . .

3   ADA AND THE MACHINE

On a hot day in May 1833, Ada—now seventeen—
waited with a hundred other girls in a side room of the
palace. Music and laughter drifted in through the doors.

Outside, in the main ballroom, His Majesty King
William IV, and his wife Queen Adelaide, were entertaining **a hundred rich young men** on the lookout for
wives.

Each of the girls looked and felt like a princess.

Well, maybe there was one who didn't.

At long last the doors opened, and the girls walked
slowly toward the head of the ballroom, where the

royal couple sat. As each girl approached Their Majesties, an usher announced her name. Finally Ada's name was called and she stepped forward. A soft murmur rippled around the room. Ada was used to this. She had been a celebrity her whole life, and people still wanted to catch a glimpse of Lord Byron's daughter.

Ada curtseyed, then backed away to make room for the next young lady. You were expected not to turn your back on the king. And that was it. The king officially knew that she existed, so from then on Ada would be on the guest list for London parties and balls throughout the Season. And she'd be expected to find herself a husband at one of them, because that was what young ladies did.

But Ada was still only seventeen. She had other plans. She wanted to make her mark in this changing world. She just needed to find a way . . .

It just so happened that Ada's math tutor, Mary Somerville, had invited her to a party, and on June 5, 1833, Ada met the man who would become **her best friend for life**.

NOT REALLY HUSBAND MATERIAL

Ada noticed him immediately. He definitely wasn't husband material, but maybe that's why she liked him. He was rich, famous, and probably the most logical person she would ever meet:

CHARLES BABBAGE

Mathematician, scientist, astronomer, engineer, and inventor.

> Quite right, I do deserve my own box.

Job: Professor of Mathematics, Cambridge University.

Status: Wealthy—he'd inherited lots of money from his very rich dad.

Characteristics:

- So vain he'd turned down the offer of a junior knighthood (he thought he deserved better).

- So logical he even corrected poets! Future Poet Laureate, Alfred, Lord Tennyson, wrote: "*Every moment dies a man, every moment one is born.*" Babbage kindly pointed out that if this was true then the population would never increase.
  The figure "one" was wrong.

> *I believe the figure $1^1/_{16}$ will be sufficiently accurate for poetry.*

Even though **Ada was seventeen and Babbage was forty-two**, they hit it off right away. They seemed to really understand each other.

34

Babbage liked to hold parties himself, for rich and famous guests, but not the sort with dancing and music and games. There was tea, but no cake, only brown bread and butter. Also, you didn't go to Babbage's parties to have fun; you went to be interesting and interested.

Babbage was very picky about his guests. They had to have at least one of three things: intellect, beauty, or rank. Ada certainly passed that test—she had all three. **She was top of the list** for his next party, on June 17.

Ada couldn't wait. She'd heard about Babbage's little gatherings and knew exactly what to expect: they had nothing to do with husband hunting.

Babbage's Bash

Ada felt a tingle of excitement as she moved through the crowd on that warm June evening. She was accompanied by Annabella, and surrounded by some of the best-known names in the British Empire. Writers, explorers, and politicians. Soldiers, sailors, and scientists. But Ada, Babbage, and the other guests all had different ideas about what was the most interesting thing at the party.

For some of the guests, it was Ada herself. They just wanted to see the famous Lord Byron's daughter. Others wanted to examine one of Babbage's little machines. He was a great tinkerer. His latest device was a little mechanical dancer made of silver that he'd rescued from a junk shop and restored to full working order.

The movement of the dancing figure was so beautiful, so lifelike, that Babbage found it hard to shift people's attention to the real attraction. His baby—and the thing Ada had come to see, was a much, much cleverer machine that he had designed himself. Babbage kept it in a dust-free room next door. Only Ada found this the most interesting thing at the party. It might not look as beautiful as the dancer, but it actually served a purpose. She didn't know it at the time, but **this machine was going to change her life**.

It was a mass of metal wheels and cogs, more complex than any clock. This was Difference Engine No. 1 and, at the time, it was **the most remarkable machine in the world**.

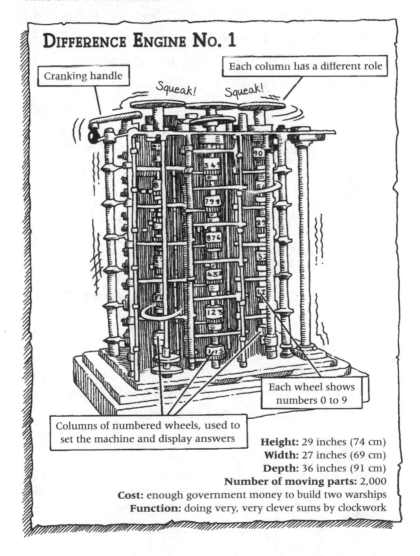

DIFFERENCE ENGINE NO. 1

Cranking handle

Each column has a different role

Squeak! Squeak!

Each wheel shows numbers 0 to 9

Columns of numbered wheels, used to set the machine and display answers

Height: 29 inches (74 cm)
Width: 27 inches (69 cm)
Depth: 36 inches (91 cm)
Number of moving parts: 2,000
Cost: enough government money to build two warships
Function: doing very, very clever sums by clockwork

THE BEAUTIFUL MACHINE

Machines and buildings were getting bigger and better, so engineers needed more and more complicated calculations to get them right. Those calculations had to be absolutely accurate, on first try. When it came to building a ship or a bridge, if just one number in a calculation was a little bit wrong, a structure could collapse.

Maximum load 3000 tons

Maximum load 300 tons

You copied the figures wrong!

This is where the Difference Engine came in. A human would get a few calculations right, but as the pressure increased, sooner or later they'd make a mistake. Babbage believed that only a machine could be **guaranteed to get every answer exactly right**.

Some people thought the Difference Engine was just a fancy calculator, but it was much cleverer than that. The trouble was, before **it** could work out the complicated calculations, **you** had to do some simple calculations first.

ADA EXPLAINS: THE DIFFERENCE ENGINE

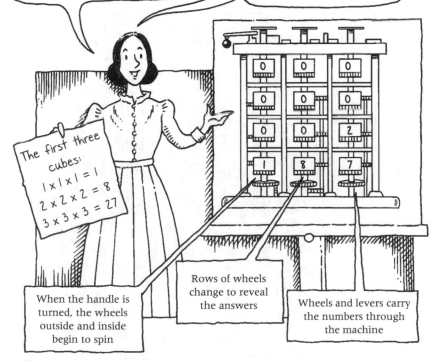

I've started by cubing some numbers. For example, three cubed is 3 x 3 x 3 = 27

I've worked out the first few cubes and I've set the wheels of the Difference Engine to show the answers.

The first three cubes:
1 x 1 x 1 = 1
2 x 2 x 2 = 8
3 x 3 x 3 = 27

When the handle is turned, the wheels outside and inside begin to spin

Rows of wheels change to reveal the answers

Wheels and levers carry the numbers through the machine

The Difference Engine looked at the differences between the human's answers (hence the name) and worked out the calculation that produced them, all by clockwork. Then, it could use the same calculation to work out bigger and bigger numbers.

So, the only limit is the number of wheels—and the operator's ability to do simple math!

However, Difference Engine No. 1 was just a demonstration model, a smaller version of a much larger design Babbage was supposed to be working on. The new machine would be steam-powered, clockwork, and able to handle even bigger numbers.

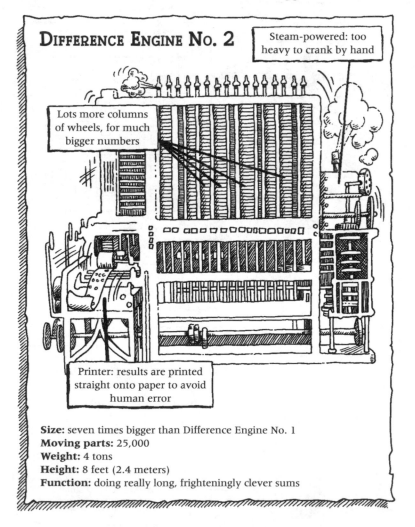

DIFFERENCE ENGINE No. 2

Steam-powered: too heavy to crank by hand

Lots more columns of wheels, for much bigger numbers

Printer: results are printed straight onto paper to avoid human error

Size: seven times bigger than Difference Engine No. 1
Moving parts: 25,000
Weight: 4 tons
Height: 8 feet (2.4 meters)
Function: doing really long, frighteningly clever sums

The British government was taking Babbage's idea very seriously. They had already given him **a massive amount of money** for research—enough to build two warships—but Babbage had spent most of that developing Difference Engine No. 1. Meanwhile, the government was kind of hoping he would actually produce Difference Engine No. 2 any day now.

Unfortunately, Babbage had the same problems as many geniuses:

- He was a perfectionist. Playing around with the idea, tinkering with it, making it absolutely right, was far more interesting than actually finishing the job.

- Babbage liked to be the boss, and his social skills weren't great. His chief engineer on the Difference Engine was a brilliant designer called Joseph Clement. One reason they stopped working together was because Babbage treated him like, well, a servant.

Milk and two sugars, please.

One of the best engineering minds in the country

If Babbage could understand something, he couldn't for the life of him see why everyone else didn't.

Some of the best minds in the country

But, Mr Babbage, how exactly does it work?

I'm very glad you asked that! *Whatever number is found upon the column of first differences will be added to the number found upon the table column. The same first difference remaining upon its own column, the number found upon the column of second differences will be added to that first difference . . .*

Ada was only seventeen, but she understood Babbage, and she understood the Difference Engine. She could have explained it much better than Babbage did—if anyone had asked.

No one at Babbage's party—apart from Babbage himself—would have taken her seriously if she'd spoken her thoughts out loud, but she immediately knew that **this machine was the future**. It made so many things possible.

Ada didn't know exactly what the future held, but from that moment on, she definitely wanted to be part of it. Finally, **she knew what she wanted to do with her life**. She had always enjoyed studying math anyway.

4   ADA ON A MISSION

Now Ada knew where she was heading, she needed to work on her math skills—she was nowhere near the world-class level of Babbage. So, she made sure she had the very **best math tutors around**, even though aristocratic ladies weren't supposed to bother themselves with such a complex subject. Ada's tutor Mary was a lady, and she was brilliant at math; she just wasn't wealthy enough to be aristocratic.

MARY SOMERVILLE
1780-1872

- Hardly went to school.

- Only really started studying math in her late twenties, but by the time she died, she was known as "the Queen of Nineteenth-Century Science."

- Taught herself by solving math problems in magazines and reading lots and lots of books.

- Also branched out into subjects like astronomy, chemistry, and physics.

- Wrote her own highly acclaimed science books.

- Has an asteroid named after her; and a crater on the Moon; and Somerville College in Oxford, England, one of the university's first all-women colleges.

Other tutors could only teach her by letter, which was a bit like virtual learning but much, much slower. Mary, however, was able to tutor Ada in person.

While she was studying, Ada kept in touch with Babbage and followed all the news about the Difference Engine, much like people today might follow a celebrity vlogger. Only, as with her tutors, it all had to be done by letter or from articles in newspapers rather than instantly, on a screen. She pestered Babbage for plans and diagrams so that she could keep up with everything he was doing.

This kept Ada busy enough to put off finding a husband for a couple more years.

All Change Up North

Meanwhile, Annabella tried to keep Ada busy with other things. In 1834, she took her on a tour of towns and cities in the north of England and the Midlands, where the Industrial Revolution was in full swing. Areas that had been farmland 100 years earlier were now **totally transformed** by industry. Factories and mills had sprung up, thanks to new steam-powered technology, and they churned out textiles and made machines that were sold worldwide.

This was a really exciting time to be alive . . . if you had money. Once upon a time, most things had been made in small workshops or at home by hand, but now **machines in factories were taking over**. Businesses got rich because they could make more goods and pay fewer people (and the government benefited by collecting taxes from them).

The workers who kept their jobs weren't paid much, and many now had no work at all. If you wanted a job—even a low-paid one—you had to go to cities, like Birmingham and Manchester, which were becoming huge.

Annabella cared deeply about social justice, and she hoped that by taking Ada to see these factories for herself, her daughter would care too. But, aside from getting away from the Furies, Ada was most interested in the **scientific developments**. She found a visit to a cloth factory in Coventry especially interesting.

A Code in the Card

The factory was hot, crowded, and noisy. It was packed to the rafters with fast-moving machinery, and men, women, and children working twelve or more hours a day.

Ada and Annabella worked their way through the rows of spinning machinery, carefully pulling their wide skirts out of reach of whirling cogs and levers. One slip in a place like this could be lethal—limbs often ended up mangled or even lopped off altogether.

The foreman demonstrated one of the latest looms and the two women watched with amazement as the machine wove a complicated pattern onto a piece of cloth, all by itself! He handed each of them a slim rectangle of tough cardboard, with rows of holes punched into it. It looked like there was some kind of pattern or code in the holes, but it was impossible to tell what.

Ada's heart pounded with excitement. This was a Jacquard card. She had in her hands an example of **the first ever machine-readable technology**! Babbage had told her about them—they could make a machine *think* for itself. She hadn't understood what he meant before, but now it all fell into place.

This is a Jacquard card. Doesn't look like much does it? But here's what it can do . . .

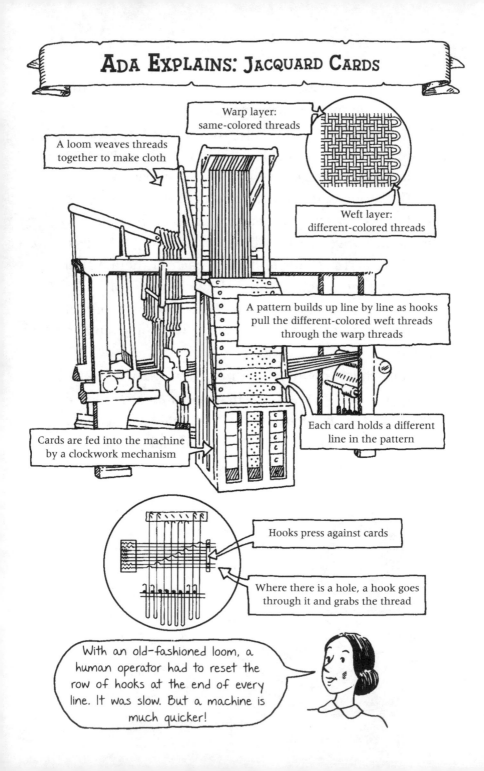

A Husband for Ada

Back home again, Annabella's search for a husband for Ada began in earnest. Thanks to the family name, the suitors weren't exactly rushing in—no one was in a hurry to marry the daughter of Lord Byron.

Some people thought Ada was "a beauty," but Ada herself didn't agree, and she certainly didn't act like one. She once commented that her jaw looked big enough to write the word "mathematics' on, and she dressed so plainly that one friend joked **it was hard to tell her apart from the servants**.

But Annabella was determined. She was still trying to live down the disgrace of her own marriage and she really wanted Ada to settle down with a nice, normal husband, and have lots of children.

In desperation, she even considered Babbage. He wasn't a lord, but he was rich and respectable—which was the next best thing—and the pair were already friends. On the other hand, he was old enough to be

Ada's father, he already had children, and he really wasn't interested.

Ada finally changed her mind about finding a husband when she realized that marriage could have one big plus. Until the day of her wedding, Ada had to live with her mother and **put up with her mother's awful friends**. Yes, at age nineteen, the frightful Furies were still plaguing her.

So, Ada was in a fairly receptive mood when Mary Somerville's son, Woronzow (his dad was Russian), introduced her to his friend from college, Lord William King.

William was a scientist too, interested in agriculture, and a Fellow of the Royal Society (i.e., very clever!). He was shy, and enjoyed Ada's company. He wasn't bothered by the Byron connection and happily let her continue studying math.

Ada came with £16,000 (about $1.3 million today) of Byron's money, and £14,000 (about $1.1 million today) of Annabella's and she stood to inherit her mom's money too when her mom died. She was bright, chatty, and always fun to be with.

William was actually quite a catch. There was a big age difference—he was thirty and Ada was nineteen—but neither of them minded. They met in the spring of 1835 and got married in July. To Annabella's delight, the Honorable Miss Ada Byron became Lady Ada King.

Lords and ladies, like Ada and William, usually married for money and status first. Love came second—if you were lucky.

William would now have control of all Ada's money, but he would give her £300 (about $25,000 today) a year. Not much if you have to live off it, but not bad at all if you're married to a rich lord who pays for everything else.

The new Lord and Lady King spent their honeymoon at William's favorite house (he owned several), Ashley Combe in Somerset.

Ada Passes a Test

Annabella was delighted with the match, but now came the ultimate test. Annabella had agreed, once Ada was married, that she would send her daughter all the things that Byron had left her. This included the ring he had sent the day he fled the country, an inkstand, some other trinkets, and a large, flat, square package.

Annabella was so anxious about this last item that she made sure her favorite doctor, Dr. King (no relation to William), was "just visiting" when Ada opened it.

Ada probably guessed it was the painting that had hung behind a curtain the whole time she'd lived with her mother. Now, with her husband by her side, she tore the package open and **saw the face of her father** for the first time since she was one month old.

Ada seemed quite calm. She didn't rush off to write any poems; in fact, she didn't react the way Annabella had dreaded at all.

She shrugged, and looked around for somewhere to hang the picture. A satisfied Dr. King reported to Annabella that Ada was OK.

He might have spoken too soon.

Four Shillings Down

In October 1835, the newlyweds spent a few days apart for the first time in their three-month-long marriage. Ada took a break with Annabella in Southampton—at the horse races.

When she was very little, Ada had been afraid of horses. But she'd overcome her fear and discovered that riding actually helped her with the nervous attacks she'd had ever since that early bout of measles, in 1829. Now she loved to gallop around the estate. So, a day in horsey company seemed like a great idea.

Horse racing was heavily tied up with gambling, of course, and **gambling horrified Annabella**. It reminded her of Byron squandering money they didn't have. But while ladies were never supposed to gamble with cards or visit a casino, betting on horses was considered acceptable. So off they went.

Somehow, Ada became separated from Annabella in the crowd. She spotted a bookie (a man taking bets) standing next to a board, with a list of names of horses, and numbers written next to them. Horses *and* numbers? Ada was intrigued.

She had four shillings in her purse. Her heart beat a little more quickly. Somewhere, very deep inside of her, Byron might have been calling, urging her to give it a try.

Ada bet the four shillings. She guessed which horses would win. She guessed *wrong*. She lost.

Later, she told William everything, but she assured him that no way was she going to get into gambling. And, at the time, she really believed it.

KIDS AND CHOLERA

In May 1836, Ada and William's first child was born. Annabella was so happy to have a grandson that she even suggested a name for him that Ada wasn't expecting at all . . .

In September 1837, young Byron was followed by . . .

. . . and finally in July 1839, Ralph.

Shortly after little Annabella was born, Ada caught cholera, a very dangerous disease that's caused by . . . well, there's no nice way to say this. It's caused by drinking water that's contaminated with . . . poop! In those days, before modern toilets and sewers, cholera was very common and could **kill its victims within a day**. First they'd feel sick and dizzy, but within a few hours . . . well, let's just say that fluid came spurting out of every hole in the body that fluid can spurt out of, and they'd die of dehydration. Ew!

Ada was one of the lucky ones.
She recovered, but the illness
really wore her out.

Once again I was confined to bed, too fragile in mind and body to do anything. I was sooo bored!

ENTER ADA LOVELACE

At this time, Ada got the name we know her by today. In June 1838, the young Queen Victoria was crowned and a whole lot of new lordly titles were created to celebrate.

The title of Lord Lovelace had died out with Ada's distant relatives, the Noel family. Under Victoria, the title made a comeback, and William and Ada found themselves renamed and retitled.

Just call me Ada Lovelace.

Lord William King-Noel,
1st Earl of Lovelace

Lady Augusta Ada King-Noel,
Countess of Lovelace

Mesmerized by Mesmerism

For four uncomfortable years, Ada was mostly either expecting a baby, looking after a baby, or ill. There wasn't much time left over for studying. Maybe that was why, though she loved her children, **she found it hard to like them**. They distracted her from her first love—mathematics. Then she found something that fascinated her so much she was able to combine her illness with study.

German scientist Franz Mesmer believed there was an invisible force that could improve human health. He called this force animal magnetism, or mesmerism (a bit like hypnotism today, with a bit of psychology thrown in), and his experimental cures began **causing quite a stir** in Europe. In the 1830s, mesmerism began to take off in England, stirring up a "mesmerism mania." Ada was fascinated too; she watched demonstrations and tried some experiments, including a famous one called the Oscillating Shilling, which demonstrated invisible forces.

Ada stared at a coin in a glass without letting anything else distract her.

Ada's thumb and finger started to tingle, and the coin began to move back and forth. It picked up speed until it was violently swinging around the glass, hitting the sides.

The coin stopped when Ada put the glass down. Every time she tried the experiment again it moved more slowly until eventually it stopped altogether.

Ultimately, Ada found that mesmerism did give her some pain relief, but didn't really help her recover. She got better the more traditional way: with lots of rest. She didn't completely rule mesmerism out, though.

BACK TO WORK

Ada finally felt well enough to return to math in 1840. She was twenty-four and Ralph was four months old. She had kept up her friendship with Babbage all this time—and started to have ideas of her own.

She and Babbage had both thought of the Difference Engine as no more than a very clever calculating machine that helped engineers do complicated equations. Babbage still thought this, but Ada was starting to see—very faintly—how math could help us with the kind of things our computers do today. Ada's imagination, which Annabella had tried so hard to erase, was making larger and larger leaps, turning Ada into **a true visionary**. She had no idea how ahead of her time she was. Sadly, neither did anyone else.

So science can be used to design things! Very interesting.

A TREATISE ON MECHANICS, APPLIED TO THE ARTS

Including Statics and Hydrostatics

Solitaire has thousands of possible outcomes.

Meanwhile, science was still churning out new device after new device. The latest wonder-invention was the electric telegraph—the closest the nineteenth century came to texting, or online shopping. An electric pulse sent a coded message along a wire, which could be received at the other end of the wire.

A letter from London would take **at least a day** to reach Ada, whereas a telegram arrived the same day (though it did have to be delivered by hand from the telegraph office). That would make it easy for Ada to place an order or let William know she'd missed her train.

Ada realized that bringing to life all the amazing gadgets that were making the world an easier place to live required a combination of scientific knowledge and a creative mind. She called this combination "poetical science."

The world was so exciting that Ada actually worried that it might all get too much for her. By now, she was pretty certain she *had* an imagination, despite Annabella's efforts, though perhaps it was becoming a little too active. A feeling had been growing inside Ada for some time, and it was this:

My desire to be a mathematician came from above.

By exploring math and science Ada felt she could help other people to understand God's creations, and even understand God himself. She just had to find a way to carry out her mission . . .

Which is where Babbage came in. While Ada had been having babies, he'd been working on a huge steel baby of his own. It would be **bigger and better** than the Difference Engine, and her work on it with him would eventually make Ada famous.

5   ANALYTICAL ADA

Babbage was worried that his beloved Difference Engine just wasn't good enough. It was slow. You had to know some of the answers in advance to make it work out the rest—and if the human got those first answers wrong, so did the machine. You had to reset it at the end of every calculation. It didn't have a memory, so you couldn't reuse a number without entering it by hand. And worst of all . . .

It can be **inaccurate!**

Even if the human operator got their calculations exactly right, there were some numbers the Difference Engine just couldn't handle. For instance, what is 1 divided by 3? The answer is 1/3, but the Difference Engine couldn't say that. It would have to say 0.3, but that answer is only *almost* right. Multiply it back again, and the answer you get is 0.9, not 1. The *real* answer is 0.3333333 etc.—which is a recurring decimal, and the Difference Engine couldn't handle recurring decimals. It ran out of wheels. But those teeny-tiny differences in the numbers could lead to **absolutely humungous** ones later on.

Difference Engine No. 2 was meant to be bigger and better than Difference Engine No. 1, but it had exactly the same problems. Babbage wasn't about to give up, though, oh no! He started devising **a whole new machine** instead.

Plans for the Analytical Engine

Designed by: C. Babbage Esq.
Weight: 4 tons, about the same as a small railway engine.
Dimensions: 15 feet high (4.5 meters). Length depends on number of columns in the Store, but at least 10 feet (3 meters).
Moving parts: 20,000 wheels and many more levers, gears and switches.
Power source: steam, of course—it was too heavy to crank by hand.

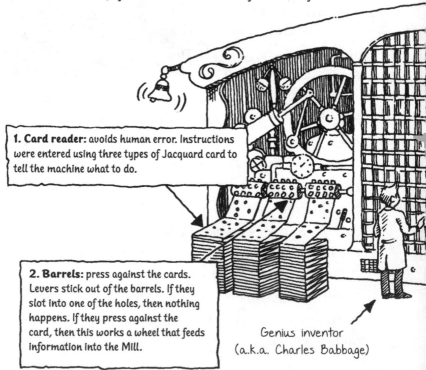

1. Card reader: avoids human error. Instructions were entered using three types of Jacquard card to tell the machine what to do.

2. Barrels: press against the cards. Levers stick out of the barrels. If they slot into one of the holes, then nothing happens. If they press against the card, then this works a wheel that feeds information into the Mill.

Genius inventor (a.k.a. Charles Babbage)

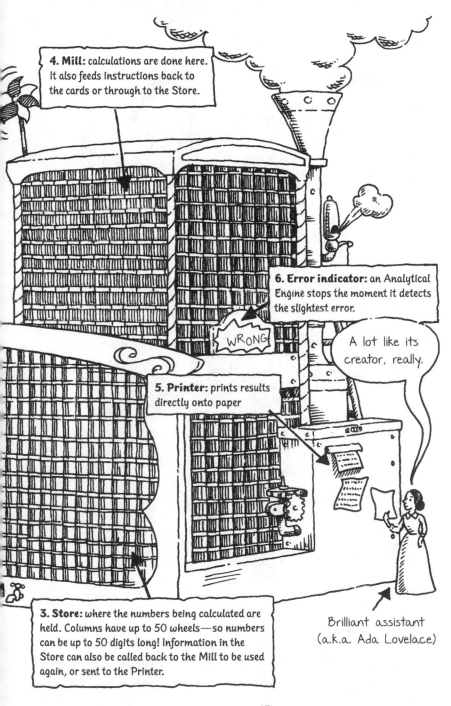

4. Mill: calculations are done here. It also feeds instructions back to the cards or through to the Store.

6. Error indicator: an Analytical Engine stops the moment it detects the slightest error.

A lot like its creator, really.

WRONG

5. Printer: prints results directly onto paper

3. Store: where the numbers being calculated are held. Columns have up to 50 wheels—so numbers can be up to 50 digits long! Information in the Store can also be called back to the Mill to be used again, or sent to the Printer.

Brilliant assistant (a.k.a. Ada Lovelace)

Sound Familiar?

The Analytical Engine had a memory. It could process numbers. It could even work on its own! Sound familiar?

Babbage only called his machine the Analytical Engine because the word *computer* meant something slightly different. In those days a computer wasn't a thing, it was a human being paid to do very complicated calculations, or computations . . .

Teams of (usually) men were employed to do different kinds of calculations.

Working out orbits of the Moon.

Working out how much the Earth wobbles as it spins.

Producing a table of high and low tides around the world for next year.

Put the answers to lots of small calculations together and you can answer much larger calculations—probably the only time a roomful of men will come up with something useful.

The Analytical Engine could do those large sums all on its own. It had hardware (the Mill, the Store, the Barrels) and software (the cards). It might have been mechanical and steam-powered, but the Analytical Engine was actually a clockwork computer: **the first computer ever designed**, and over 100 years ahead of its time!

It was amazing, and it wasn't just good for number-crunching—Ada saw so many other ways it could be used. The Analytical Engine could make Britain a world leader in science, in art, in engineering—in any field you can think of. There was just one small problem. Like the Difference Engine No. 2, the Analytical Engine **didn't actually exist** . . . yet.

Building it would take money. (Babbage was a very rich man, but he wasn't *that* rich.) The British government had already given him a lot of money, and all Babbage had produced was a demonstration model. So they wouldn't be coughing up any more cash without a very good reason.

Babbage needed to find another way to pay for his Analytical Engine. People needed to know about it and understand what it could do, the difference it could make. **It needed publicity**.

Babbage definitely wasn't the person to do this. He had horrible people skills and *really* couldn't handle stupid questions.

Whoever tried to publicize the Analytical Engine would have to answer a lot of questions, many of them stupid.

Babbage needed someone who understood:

a) him;

b) the Analytical Engine; and

c) other people.

It was the perfect job for Ada. She just had to decide how she was going to do it.

6   ADA MAKES SOME NOTES

In fall 1840, just as Ada was taking up math again, Babbage was invited to Turin, Italy, to talk to some Italian scientists about the Analytical Engine. The Italians loved him and he loved them. They treated Babbage as a great mathematician, scientist, and engineer, which was exactly how he thought he should be treated back in England (and wasn't).

One of the scientists, Luigi Federico Menabrea, was so impressed by Babbage's talk that he wrote and published an article about it in October 1842.

The article was pretty much word for word what Babbage had said in his Turin speech, so he got the details right, but Ada found it . . . disappointing. Menabrea had copied Babbage so carefully that the article **hardly made any sense** to a non-genius, i.e., most anyone. Besides, it had been published in a European journal, in French. This wouldn't help Ada publicize the Analytical Engine, but it did give her an idea.

I speak French. I'll translate the article and publish it in English!

But it still won't make sense to most people.

Then I'll just add a couple of notes at the end.

Ada Becomes Note-orious

Babbage couldn't understand why Ada didn't just write her own article. Ada didn't do that because . . . um . . . well, to be honest, it just didn't occur to her. In the end, Ada's Notes (and they deserve a capital N) were two and a half times longer than the article!

She wrote seven Notes in total. By now, most scientists and mathematicians had heard of the Difference Engine, so first they needed to know what made the Difference Engine and the Analytical Engine, er . . . different.

This is, roughly, how Ada explained it in Note A:

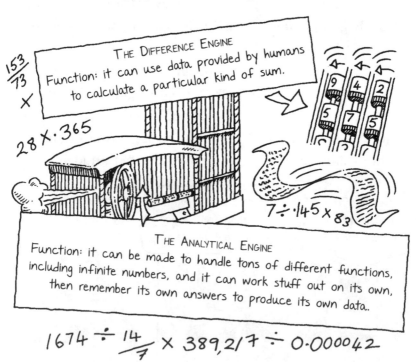

THE DIFFERENCE ENGINE
Function: it can use data provided by humans to calculate a particular kind of sum.

THE ANALYTICAL ENGINE
Function: it can be made to handle tons of different functions, including infinite numbers, and it can work stuff out on its own, then remember its own answers to produce its own data.

Even Babbage was impressed when he read Note A.

It demonstrates a depth of understanding that even I did not anticipate.

Babbage still thought of the Analytical Engine as just a massive, and massively impressive, calculating machine that would help Victorian bridge-building engineers, ship designers, and steam-engine manufacturers get their figures exactly right.

But Ada approached it with **poetical science**. By combining her scientific knowledge and understanding with her imagination, she saw things differently:

My Analytical Engine can perform any calculation you care to name with perfect accuracy.

I agree, but it could also be used to draw pictures and design sculptures and buildings and statues and compose music and—

Music? Art? What nonsense!

Well, in Ada's mind, music was just a series of different sounds, put together mathematically.

Notes progress in a pattern, which is another way of saying they're a mathematical sequence.

Pictures could be broken down into **mathematically described shapes and colors**. If something was mathematical—and almost everything is—then the Analytical Engine could handle it.

Pictures can be divided into areas that are proportionate to each other in size.

The Analytical Engine weaves algebraic patterns just as the Jacquard loom weaves flowers and leaves.

Even Babbage, who had had the idea for this amazing machine, didn't get Ada's way of thinking. He may have invented the computer, but **it was Ada who realized what computers could do**. In the middle of the nineteenth century, Ada Lovelace had just invented the idea of digital music and computer graphics. OK, so there was no computer advanced enough to play them on, but even so—WOW!

THINK OF A NUMBER SEQUENCE

In Note B, Ada described how the Analytical Engine's hardware, the Store and Mill, worked—and right away she introduced her readers to a whole new concept. Until now, all the cogs and wheels of mechanical machines—from a basic clock to the Difference Engine, and anything in between—were designed to do just one job. But in the Analytical Engine, all those cogs and wheels could be made to do *different* things, often at the same time. That was amazing enough on its own, but what was even more amazing was that they **didn't need a human** to tell them what to do. The machine could do its own thinking.

Ada just needed a killer demonstration to show what the Analytical Engine was capable of. She thought of the most difficult calculation she could set . . . the most complicated mathematical pattern it could weave.

Bernoulli numbers are so ridiculously, ludicrously complex that Ada didn't fully understand them and even the Difference Engine couldn't manage them. She had to ask Babbage for the *extremely* complicated equation that is normally used.

Here's part of the Bernoulli equation. See what I mean?

$$\frac{x}{e^x-1} = \sum_{n=0}^{\infty} B_n \frac{x^n}{n!}$$

So now, for Note G, she had the **incredibly challenging** task of making the Analytical Engine calculate Bernoulli numbers. First, she had to make the equation understandable to the Analytical Engine, and then she had to make it understandable to the average reader, so they would get what she was doing.

Today, mathematicians use Bernoulli numbers to calculate how air flows over and under airplane wings in flight.

I wish I'd known that when I was designing my flying machine . . .

Ada's Input

Writing the Notes meant that, for the first time, Ada gave Babbage's plans for the Analytical Engine a long, hard look with her analytical mind. Whenever she spotted an error, Ada fed it back to Babbage so that Babbage could improve the design. At one point, she noticed an error in the mechanism for working out equations; at another, she realized Babbage was wrong about the number of cards needed. Together, Ada and Babbage polished up the idea of the Analytical Engine and **made it even better**.

Ada was enjoying herself! But if she'd had her way, her contribution would have been the Analytical Engine's best-kept secret.

Ada didn't want her name on the article because

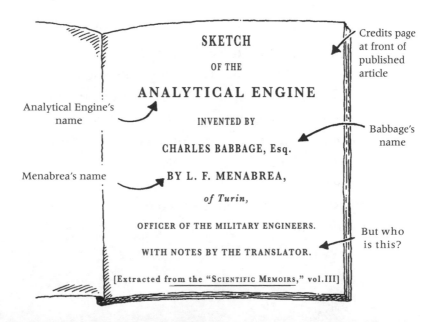

Credits page at front of published article

Analytical Engine's name

Babbage's name

Menabrea's name

But who is this?

SKETCH

OF THE

ANALYTICAL ENGINE

INVENTED BY

CHARLES BABBAGE, Esq.

BY L. F. MENABREA,

of Turin,

OFFICER OF THE MILITARY ENGINEERS.

WITH NOTES BY THE TRANSLATOR.

[Extracted from the "SCIENTIFIC MEMOIRS," vol.III]

she still saw herself as **Babbage's humble servant**. As with her dad's bestselling poem, she didn't want to get rich on the back of the article, because lords and ladies were not supposed to earn money. Additionally, the Lovelace family motto was *Labor ipse voluptas*— "Labor is its own reward."

But even though he was a lord, William thought Ada should take the credit. She was the one who had made the translation, after all. The Notes could be the first step in her mathematical career, he pointed out— but only if Ada admitted she'd written them. It was just publicity; no money would be changing hands so it didn't count as paid work.

In the end, Ada reluctantly signed each page of the Notes with her initials, A. A. L.

Note G

Ada worked on the translation and the Notes for nearly a year, but Note G is the one she's most remembered for, because it's where she broke the Bernoulli equation down into lots of simpler equations. She put each one into a row of a table. Running a number through each of the simpler equations in turn would give the same result as using the full equation from the start. Ada's system worked just like a team of human computers.

Her table looked something like this:

Ada just called her table a table. But to modern eyes, it's a list of machine-readable instructions. Ada had gone and written **the world's first ever computer program**! Which made Ada Lovelace, an aristocratic lady living in Victorian England, the world's first computer programmer!

THE BABBAGE FACTOR

Babbage was 100 percent behind Ada, and gave her a lot of helpful advice. But working with him still wasn't easy. In fact, thanks to him, the Notes very nearly didn't get published. Babbage was so absent-minded that he managed to lose some of the pages when Ada sent them to him for approval. Ada was so angry she nearly forgot she was a lady!

This was long before photocopiers had been invented, so Ada had to **rewrite the whole thing from memory**.

Then Babbage decided he wanted to write a preface (or introduction) to the article, to tell everyone what it was about. Ada thought that would be fine, since the machine was his baby. She must have forgotten what Babbage was like . . . until she read what he had written. All those little irritations that had built up over the years, especially his treatment by the British government, had come pouring out.

To top it all off, he asked Ada to sign what he'd written, so **it would look like she had written it** herself! Ada refused point-blank. She said it would be suicidal. Babbage threatened to pull the whole article . . . It was nearly the end of their friendship.

But ultimately, it was Ada's article, not Babbage's. So she left his preface out. The article and the Notes were published in September 1843, in a journal called *Scientific Memoirs*. Babbage's ranty piece was published in another magazine.

And that was it. A whole year of hard work all done. Even Babbage was impressed enough to stop sulking and gush with praise.

> *She is the Enchantress of Number. She has thrown her magical spell around mathematics and has grasped it with a force that few masculine intellects could have exerted.*

In other words, he thought she was brilliant with numbers and even better than most men! So now Ada could sit back and enjoy fame and fortune, while the Analytical Engine finally got built, ushering in the Computer Age in the middle of the nineteenth century. Right? *Wrong.*

7   AGENT ADA

Unfortunately, on the November 11, 1842, eleven months before the Notes were published, Babbage had met with the prime minister of Great Britain to try to persuade him to fund his new machine. **The meeting had not gone well**.

Prime Minister Sir Robert Peel. Not the greatest fan of the Analytical Engine or its inventor.

The machine's only value is to work out exactly how useless it is.

Meeting set up by Prince Albert, Queen Victoria's husband, and a great believer in technology.

Convincing Sir Robert was never going to be easy. He was a busy man, and he had already made up his mind on the Analytical Engine very clear indeed. But there was still a chance the meeting could have worked.

Here's how Ada would have handled it:

We've had some terrible harvests, so food prices are high. There could be a famine!

Fear not, Prime Minister, the Analytical Engine can help you organize agriculture and plan food distribution.

I want to limit child labor without losing out on profits from our industries. Factory workers ages nine to thirteen should work shorter hours and get a break for lunch.

The Analytical Engine could help you plan a program that's fair to workers while keeping factories prosperous.

I have an empire to run! An army! A navy!

The Analytical Engine can help work out how to get our soldiers and ships wherever they're needed! And the money you'll save will pay for the cost of the machine!

Marvellous!

Then you shall have all the funding you need, Lady Lovelace!

Here's roughly what actually happened when Babbage met the prime minister:

That was that. There was no chance of getting any money out of the government now. When Ada found out, she couldn't believe her ears. Babbage was in trouble—but she *could* see a way out.

Ada's Offer

Ada really believed that Babbage's machine could change the world, but she knew it was going to take more than his brilliant engineering skills to make it happen. So, she decided to **make him an offer he couldn't refuse**. On Monday August 14, 1843, she sat down to write the most important letter of her life.

By now, she knew how Babbage's mind worked, so she made the letter all about *him*. She talked about how brilliant he was, how busy he must be, and she suggested that he should dedicate his colossal intellect to the creation of the Analytical Engine, while she handled *everything* else. The final part of her (sixteen-page) letter boiled down to these three questions:

1. Will you let me deal with other people at all times?

> After that interview with the prime minister, the fewer people Babbage met, the better.

2. Will you deal with technical problems I identify as soon as I identify them?

> There were some technical problems only Babbage could handle, but he had a habit of ignoring everyone else's concerns. I needed him to answer any questions I raised.

3. If I come up with a publicity plan for the Analytical Engine, will you back it all the way?

> I knew I could skillfully direct his time and energy; I just needed him to follow that direction. Easier said than done with Babbage!

Ada would flatter and charm people, instead of becoming hostile. She had social skills enough for the two of them. No one ever left a meeting with Ada feeling angry and upset (apart from Babbage). She'd find backers prepared to give them the money to build the Analytical Engine. She would make sure cash was always available when it was needed. She would direct his engineers, and make sure they were happy in their work.

In short, **Ada was offering to become Babbage's agent**, a project manager for every part of his life, helping to make the Analytical Engine become real. And what's more—because *Labor ipse voluptas*—he wouldn't have to pay her a penny.

Ada made the offer with great visions for the future, secretly hoping she'd eventually be able to start pointing the Analytical Engine at non-mathematical problems, like art and music—maybe even poetry.

The Computer Age was just around the corner. Ada could feel it coming. This had to be the mission that God had given her and she was absolutely ready to throw herself at it. She just needed Babbage to say yes.

Babbage didn't write back. He went to see Ada in person the very next day. She was so nervous. She expected some discussion, maybe some fine-tuning of her conditions into something Babbage felt he could work with.

Babbage's diary for the next day states his answer very bluntly.

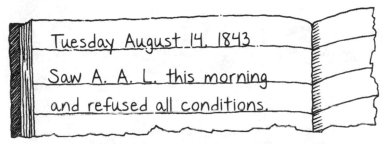

Tuesday August 14, 1843
Saw A. A. L. this morning and refused all conditions.

But why? We know Babbage totally trusted Ada's mathematical abilities, or he wouldn't have called her the "Enchantress of Number." We know he thought her Notes were brilliant, but maybe that was the problem. From now on, if people didn't understand what he was talking about, Babbage could just point them in the direction of the Notes, and bingo! He wouldn't need Ada to convince them to pay for his machine once they understood his genius.

And all the other possibilities Ada saw for the Analytical Engine—the art, the music, etc.—well, Babbage just didn't get them.

Ada was **incredibly disappointed** by his answer, but she didn't give up hope right away. After all, no one had actually read her Notes yet—the article hadn't been published. Maybe that would help. She'd just have to wait for publication day.

Slowly, September 1843 came around . . .

But She's Just a Woman!

The Notes were a work of genius. They showed that the author had a brilliant mathematical mind. But people didn't **realize** who the author was right away. When they did, some quickly changed their tune:

Thankfully, Babbage himself told people outright that Ada hadn't just written the Notes—she'd actually corrected some of his mistakes too!

And I wouldn't say that if I didn't mean it!

Luckily, many of the people who mattered—the scientists and mathematicians—read the Notes, and nodded in agreement.

In the end, though, it didn't matter how great Ada said the Analytical Engine *could* be. If the machine didn't exist, it wouldn't do any of the brilliant things she'd explained. Now that Babbage had ruined things with the Prime Minister and refused Ada's offer—well, it looked highly unlikely that the machine would ever exist.

ADA DEPRESSED

With all Ada's hope and optimism crushed, her illness made a sudden comeback. Her weight went up and down, and her physical and mental health just kept on going *down*.

From the outside, apart from the disappointment of the Analytical Engine, **Ada's life looked practically perfect.** She was still young—not even thirty yet. She had three fine children and a husband who loved her.

She had her music and her horse riding. She had her pets—a pair of dogs, Sprite and Nelson, and a collection of birds—that she loved so much she let them roam freely around the house.

She moved in high society, with rich and amazing friends: writers like William Wordsworth and Charles Dickens, famous people like the Duke of Wellington, and scientists like Michael Faraday.

But Ada desperately wanted to be part of the new age of scientific discovery, and it seemed she was being left behind. **She grew so depressed** that her mind felt as paralyzed as her body had been when she was a child. Why couldn't she *do* anything?

Soon, her home life wasn't going too well either. After ten years of marriage, William still let her pursue her studies, still gave her an allowance, and still really loved her. Ada desperately wanted to love him back, but **the spark just wasn't there**, and there was nothing William could do about it. It wasn't his fault, though, Ada had never really wanted a husband in the first place. The children hadn't improved things either. When they were little, Ada had loved them without liking them. Now that she was ill again, she even had difficulty loving them.

Unfortunately, every year adds to my utter want of pleasure in my children. They are to me irksome duties, and nothing more.

A modern doctor would probably say that Ada was suffering from depression, which can affect the body as well as the mind. When her regular doctor visited at the end of 1844, he said she had "a mad look" so horrible that he would never forget it and he immediately prescribed her twenty-five drops of laudanum, a foul-tasting mixture of opium and wine that reduced pain, but also took away the patient's ability to think clearly.

Today's doctors would never dream of prescribing such a harmful and addictive drug for depression, but on this occasion, strangely, the laudanum seemed to work. After a year of nothing happening, Ada felt able to take control of her thoughts again.

When Life Gives You Lemons . . .

In fact, Ada started to wonder whether her illness was the answer. Soon after her recovery, **she had her next great idea**.

If scientists could map the planets and their movements, maybe they could map the human mind too?

Well, she could be the first to try . . .

CALCULUS OF THE NERVOUS SYSTEM

Or, a mathematical map of the human mind
Outline of ideas by Ada Lovelace

Question: How do thoughts and feelings arise in the brain?

Answer: We don't know.

We believe that:

All things are made of atoms.

Atoms are held together by by electric and magnetic forces.

Therefore so is the brain.

Can the two somehow work together??

Aim: To create a mathematical model of how the brain works

Materials: The laboratory of my mind—i.e., my own brain

I shall work out a law or laws for the mutual actions of the molecules of the brain.

It was a great idea and it shows just how unstoppable Ada was when she put her mind to it, but, over 150 years later, even with modern medical imaging, scientists **still aren't "brainy" enough to work it out**.

Mystical, Mesmerizing Magnetism

While Ada's thoughts were in this direction, she wondered if mesmerism was worth another look. The practice was all about invisible forces, and whatever it was that made the brain work had to be an invisible force too. She hadn't given mesmerism much thought since she'd recovered from cholera, but it definitely interested her now.

If mesmerism was real, Ada reckoned it probably had something to do with electricity. Victorian scientists knew that electric currents run along the body's nerves and make muscles work because of an experiment by Italian scientist Luigi Galvani.

Ada wanted to properly test mesmerism, and she thought she knew how. She decided to write an article on the German scientist Karl von Reichenbach, who claimed that some mesmerized patients produced "luminous emanations" when they were exposed to magnetism—in other words, **they glowed**!

So many of the claims about mesmerism were impossible to prove, but Ada thought this one could be tested. If a patient *said* she was feeling better, she may not be telling the truth, but, *if* mesmerism made her glow, anyone could see it.

Science says that if something is scientifically true then it is **always** true, no exceptions, it doesn't matter who says otherwise, and you can prove it by experimenting. You can say, in advance, "If I do THIS, then THAT will happen," and it does.

Ada wanted to test Reichenbach's claim using a new sort of science that was just taking off: **the science of photography**.

Stop talking and hold that pose for another five minutes . . .

People were actually managing to capture images and store them on bits of glass or paper or metal treated with certain chemicals—it was incredible!

A photograph should show whether people glowed during mesmerism and then the amount of light could be measured and graded. Mesmerism could be put to the test once and for all.

It was a great idea, but sadly Ada's article was never published, and, as far as we know, no one ever tried her experiment. Something positive did come from it, though. Ada suddenly felt a whole lot better. Focusing on a serious piece of science—the thing she enjoyed more than anything else—had improved her health dramatically. Her depression lifted and, wonderfully, she found she could actually enjoy being a mom again!

So it's kind of a shame that after years and years of having very good ideas, her new energy and purpose now brought mostly **seriously awful ones**.

8 ADA AND THE HORSES

By 1845, it was pretty clear that **Ada's future did not include the Analytical Engine**. Without funding, and without Ada's project management, Babbage's work on it had totally stalled.

Science was still Ada's religion. She still felt she was on a mission from God, but she was having difficulty figuring out what He wanted her to do next. So she tried a few things out . . .

Before marrying William, Ada had experimented with a design for a women's swimsuit. Women didn't really go swimming in those days—they just waded out into the water, paddled about a bit, and waded back—and there was a good reason for that . . .

Usual swimsuit:
- Petticoats fill up with air. If the lower half starts to float, the woman falls over.
- Impossible to swim in.

One-piece suit designed by Ada:
- No inflating petticoats.
- Swimming is possible.

It was a practical idea, but Ada's future definitely did not lie in fashion design.

Perhaps William could help. He'd written an article about growing crops, and Ada added some technical footnotes about using a nebulometer, which was a machine for measuring daylight.

But working with William was nowhere near as exciting as working out a program for a clockwork computer. She had a brilliant mind, and she wanted to use it. For Ada, it was numbers or nothing!

She'd been friends with Babbage for over ten years now and even though things hadn't worked out with the Analytical Engine, the two of them still loved to talk about math and bounce ideas off each other. Years earlier, Ada had discussed the math of Solitaire, a game for one player that involves moving pegs on a board until only one is left. Ada thought she could create a language that would apply math to games so she could **win any game by working it out mathematically**.

She was thinking **way ahead of everyone else**, again, having ideas that that wouldn't be realized for another century. Little did she know that one day a computer language would be named after her, which would do far more important stuff than playing games.

While Ada was thinking about Solitaire, Babbage had vague plans for something like an automatic tic-tac-toe machine. It would have been the first ever gadget where you could enter a move and the machine would play against you. It could have been the ancestor to today's handheld games!

Step right up. A penny a game!

There are 26,830 possible games that can be played on this grid.

No thanks, it's easier with chalk and pavement.

Babbage thought he might raise money for the Analytical Engine by displaying the games machine at fairs, and offering members of the public the chance to play on it. Ada encouraged him, hoping his machine would *produce the silver and golden somethings*—enough money, in other words—to develop the Analytical Engine further.

Sadly, their gaming ideas didn't pan out. Babbage's butterfly mind fluttered off in yet another new direction, and Ada had other things to worry about. She hadn't been joking about those silver and golden somethings. Money was starting to press on her mind . . .

Money, Money, Money

Despite ten years of marriage, William still gave Ada the same allowance of £300 each year (about $20,000 today). It was worth a lot less by then than it had been at the start. By contrast Annabella had a far more impressive income of £7,000 a year (about $500,000 today).

Remember the four-shilling bet she'd lost way back at the horse track? **Ada hadn't forgotten the excitement of it.** Now, without the distraction of a project, the bit of Byron in her she'd tried so hard to suppress was creeping back. She started spending some of her allowance to bet on the horses.

Gambling is all down to probability, and probability is part of math. I'm very good at math, so what can possibly go wrong?

Quite a lot, actually.

How Horse Racing Works (Very Briefly)

SEACOOKIE 5-1

Bookies work out how likely Seacookie is to win. The odds on Seacookie are 5–1.

Five pounds on Seacookie, please.

If Ada bets $5 on Seacookie to win and the horse does win, she gets $25 (five times what she bet). And she gets back the $5 she paid.

But if Seacookie loses, she loses her $5.

But I know I can win next time. Just one more try . . .

And *that* was where Ada went wrong.

If Ada had inherited her father's impulse to gamble, she'd also inherited his poor choice of winners. **She kept on losing**. She lost so much that she had to borrow money from the banks to pay her debts. By 1850, she owed the banks £500 (about $35,000 today), which was £200 more than her annual income. So she borrowed a few hundred from Annabella to pay the bank back.

I . . . er . . . need it for my . . . er . . . traveling fund.

Taking a Break

In 1848, maybe because of the stress of the gambling losses, **Ada's aches and pains were back**, and her heart was beating in strange, irregular ways. Today we'd say she was having palpitations. She tried various remedies, but the symptoms didn't go away.

Finally, in 1850, deciding that a break would be good for her health, William and Ada took a vacation, touring the north of England.

Among other places, they visited Newstead Abbey, in Nottinghamshire. Byron had lived there, and it was where he was buried. So, Newstead was Ada's family home, though, of course, **Annabella had never taken her there**. This was Ada's first visit, and she absolutely loved it.

Newstead was now owned by Thomas Wildman, an old school friend of Byron's, and he was more than happy to show the Lovelaces around. **He even talked to Ada about her father**, and she discovered a few things that the two of them had in common:

📎 They both enjoyed swimming. That's why Ada had designed her swimsuit. In 1810, Byron had become the first man to swim from Europe to Asia, across the Hellespont in Turkey—two and a half miles —through very treacherous water.

📎 They both sometimes had difficulty controlling their weight.

📎 They both loved animals. Ada was delighted to discover that, just like her, Byron had let animals wander around his home. Except, while Ada had a couple of dogs, a parrot, and some starlings, his menagerie had included eight dogs, some tortoises, a hedgehog, three monkeys, five cats, an eagle, a crow, a falcon—oh, and a bear.

When Byron discovered he couldn't bring his wolfhound to college, he had turned up with a bear instead.

And, as it turned out, Ada and Byron both loved Newstead.

Something in the landscape, the woods, and the great halls of the ancient building itself, seemed to speak to Ada. It was as if **her father's side of her soul was waking up**.

For years Ada had been afraid of her dad. Now, suddenly, she didn't feel scared anymore. She'd discovered he wasn't all bad. Even Annabella had to agree that he had been on the side of the poor and oppressed: the reason he'd been in Greece when he died was because he was helping the Greeks fight for their independence. Ada began to realize that she really wasn't worried about turning out like him.

The Lovelace Losers

William left Newstead to go and attend to some boring agricultural business, and Ada was left alone. She took herself to the Doncaster Racecourse, and finally threw all caution to the wind. Her favorite horse, Voltigeur, was running, and she bet on him to win—not for any clever mathematical reasons, but because he belonged to a friend. It was just the kind of thing her father would have done. And, believe it or not, **Voltigeur won**!

Next, Ada went to the Epsom Derby, one of the most important horse races of the year. The good news: she bet on Voltigeur again, and he won again. The bad news: she also backed several losers. By the end of the day **she'd lost a lot more than she'd won**.

No!!

You win some, you lose some . . .

She knew she had to tell William that she was in debt. But unfortunately, William couldn't do much to help without going to Annabella.

FEELING THE PINCH

Even though her daughter had been married for ten years, Annabella couldn't quite let go. She cunningly kept a bit of control the only way she could: by managing the couple's money.

William owned properties that were worth a lot, but getting ahold of large amounts of cash was harder than you'd think. He'd been promised plenty of money when he married Ada, but Annabella only **paid out small amounts**, bit by bit. It was enough for William and Ada to live on, but for anything extra they had to ask Annabella. Because Annabella held the family purse strings, she could tighten— or loosen—them as she pleased.

When one of the Lovelace houses needed repairs, for example, Annabella told William to pay
for the work and promised to pay him back. He hired
the workmen to do their thing, but Annabella really
took her time handing over the money.

Now Annabella was smelling a rat. She soon worked
out that her daughter was in debt, so when Ada
produced a long list of expenses, Annabella took a
long, hard look.

You spent how much
at the hairdresser's?

Ada's Expenses
Books $$$$$
Clothes $$$$$
Hairdresser $$$$$
Dentist $$$$$
Children's riding teachers $$
Travel fund $$$$$

Eventually Annabella agreed to pay for some
items, but it wasn't enough to pay off the rest of Ada's
gambling debts. In desperation, Ada hit on an idea
that would get them all their money back, big time.
It involved a bit more gambling, but the money she'd
win would be huge.

No married woman had much cash in those days, so to convince the bookies she could afford the bets, Ada needed William on her side. He just had to sign a little letter . . .

William agreed, but he was making a big mistake.

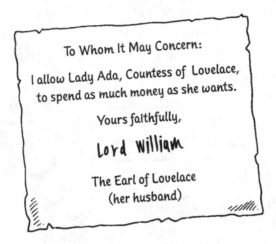

To Whom It May Concern:

I allow Lady Ada, Countess of Lovelace, to spend as much money as she wants.

Yours faithfully,

Lord William

The Earl of Lovelace
(her husband)

FOOLISHLY FOOLPROOF

Ada reckoned she'd worked out a foolproof system for winning bets. She convinced a group of five friends to join with her in a gambling syndicate. They would share what they won between them. That way, **they could spend more money on bigger bets**, and get even bigger winnings back. At least, that was the idea.

Ada was the syndicate's bookie, so she set the odds and paid out the winnings. When it came to losses, she had to pay for those herself.

The sensible thing would have been to spread the syndicate's bets over several different horses—some would lose, but others might win—then overall they wouldn't lose much money. But Ada didn't do that. Oh no. At the York Spring Meeting of 1851, she put nearly *all* the syndicate's money on her favorite horse, Voltigeur . . . and Voltigeur lost.

So, Ada's foolproof system turned out to be extremely foolish. In desperation, she tried to win all the money back at the Derby on May 21. She had just enough money left to make it work—if she won. This time she bet on several horses, just in case.

They *all* lost. Ada now owed over **ten times her annual income**. To pay that back from her allowance, she'd have to spend nothing for the next ten years and eight months!

At first, she didn't dare tell William. But soon she had to. Most of that money was owed to a man named Malcolm. Malcolm was even more broke than Ada was and he started making threats:

Ada was horrified. Everyone knew her father had been forced out of the country because of his debts. That didn't happen anymore, but still, a gentleman—or in this case, a lady—was expected to behave honorably. Ada knew she'd have to pay up, if she wanted to keep her reputation. **She had no choice but to tell William *everything*.**

After that, things became a little bit tense in the Lovelace household, to say the least. William thought through his options and agreed to pay Malcolm off. He didn't want to disgrace his wife, however foolish she'd been.

He didn't pay up right away, but he did pay eventually, so at least Ada could breathe again. And being honest about the debts brought her and William closer together. There were still tough times ahead, but she felt sure they could get through them as a couple.

Let's put it all behind us.

In fact, in the same month as her disastrous Derby losses, something happened that made her feel very positive about the future.

9 ADA'S FINAL ADVENTURE

In May 1851, Ada and William were off to the opening of the Great Exhibition in London, followed by a ball at Buckingham Palace that was hosted by Queen Victoria and Prince Albert, no less.

Exhibition featured the world's first ever pay-to-use public toilets. The cost was a penny.

TOILETS
A PENNY A GO

Hurry up!

Venue: the Crystal Palace, a 1800-foot-long glass pavilion in Hyde Park

Average daily attendance: 43,000 people, from farmworkers to lords and ladies

THE GREAT EXHIBITION

- Held May 1 to October 15, 1851 to highlight the excellence of invention and manufacturing in Britain and around the world.

- Total attendance: Six million people (one third of the population of Britain).

- Number of exhibits: 100,000 with ten miles of display space.

- Exhibits included: scientific instruments, musical instruments, works of art, and weaponry.

All the latest scientific inventions were there. The Analytical Engine should have been exhibited too, except, of course, it didn't exist. Even so, surrounded by the greatest science of the greatest country on Earth, **Ada was thrilled.**

The Crystal Palace itself was poetical science in action. It looked beautiful. Ada would have made the trip just to see it. She had read about most of the exhibits, but this was the first time she got to see the science she had learned about actually being put into use. Clever people had used their imaginations to come up with some brand-new things—it was all so exciting.

The Great Exhibition filled Ada with a new sense of hope. She was still only in her mid-thirties; there was plenty of time left for her to really make her mark. She thought that life couldn't get much better than that.

But Ada's own body had other ideas.

TERRIBLE NEWS

Just a few weeks after the Great Exhibition, Ada began to bleed for days at a time. The human body can't afford to lose too much blood, and whenever the bleeding stopped, **Ada felt drained and exhausted**.

Ada's doctor, Dr. Locock, was summoned, but she didn't want to make a fuss.

And so the treatments began:

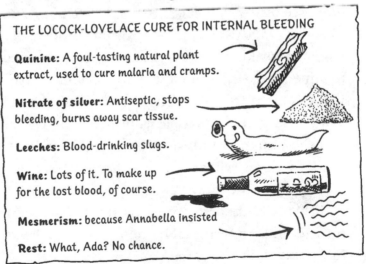

THE LOCOCK-LOVELACE CURE FOR INTERNAL BLEEDING

Quinine: A foul-tasting natural plant extract, used to cure malaria and cramps.

Nitrate of silver: Antiseptic, stops bleeding, burns away scar tissue.

Leeches: Blood-drinking slugs.

Wine: Lots of it. To make up for the lost blood, of course.

Mesmerism: because Annabella insisted

Rest: What, Ada? No chance.

But the doctor hadn't got the diagnosis quite right. There was certainly a growth, but it definitely wasn't healthy. **Ada had cancer**.

I'd rather have ten or five what I call real years of life, than twenty or thirty such as I see people usually dawdling on, without any spirit.

Once Ada realized she might not have much time left, she was determined to use every second she had. She now knew the Analytical Engine was not going to happen in her lifetime, but surely she could prove herself in some other way?

She wasn't really well enough to travel much, but she could still keep writing to Babbage and other scientists.

Dear Babs, I have an idea . . .

Sadly, Ada was suffering from cancer of the womb, and nineteenth-century medicine offered no treatment. As the pain grew worse and worse, Dr. Locock prescribed opium (another seriously dangerous painkiller) to help Ada cope. It dulled her mind so much that she couldn't think, and it was highly addictive.

Meanwhile, William made a fateful decision. Still reeling from the news about Ada's debts and now with his wife desperately ill, he needed someone to turn to and, unfortunately, he chose Annabella. **He told her everything.**

Mother Moves In

Annabella was aghast. OK, so Ada was seriously ill. She could handle that. It was the other stuff.

Addiction and gambling! So that's why she borrowed all that money.

It seemed Ada had turned out just like her father after all!

There was only one way to stop all this, Annabella decided: Ada needed her mother now more than ever. Slowly but surely, she wheedled her way into the family home until there was no getting rid of her.

Annabella wanted Ada off the opium, so she overrode the doctor's advice and called in a pair of mesmerists who waved their hands over Ada to no avail.

She also wasted no time in finding out all the facts about Ada's debts. When Anabella discovered that William had known about them all along, that was absolutely the final straw. William, she decided, was a totally unsuitable husband. From now on, **she would run Ada's life**. Dependent on Annabella for his income, William really couldn't argue.

Annabella didn't waste any time. First, she fired most of Ada's household servants and replaced them with her own. Then she fired Dr. Locock and brought in her personal doctor. At least he wasn't into mesmerism, but what he did prescribe was hardly going to help:

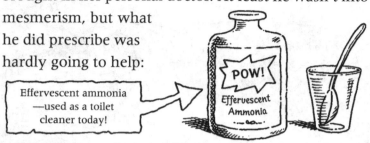

Effervescent ammonia —used as a toilet cleaner today!

None of it made any difference. By the start of 1852, Ada was living with terrible pain and was confined to a wheelchair and the ground floor of their home. One small plus, however, was that her wheelchair was fitted with the latest technology . . .

Amazingly, in August 1852 Ada managed to pose for a final portrait by Henry Phillips, the son of Thomas Phillips, who had painted the famous curtain-covered portrait of her dad. He showed her sitting at a piano, fingers on the keys, but it was clear she was ill. Her eyes and cheeks were sunken. Her arms were like sticks. She was thin and wasted from the disease.

Phillips could have painted the picture in any colors he liked, but he made it look almost like a black-and-white photo. A photo of a person at the end of her life.

The end *was* **very near** for Ada, but she stayed positive. She kept on writing to Babbage and her other friends.

10   ADA'S LAST LAUGH

Charles Babbage came to visit Ada on August 12, 1852. He had stuck by her throughout her illness and all the difficult times. By now, Ada knew she was dying and she was making preparations. There was no one she trusted more than Babbage to do what she wanted—not even William.

So Ada gave Babbage a letter with instructions for after her death.

We don't know what the projects she mentions were, and as it turned out, Babbage couldn't carry out Ada's wishes, because the letter wasn't a proper will. Babbage could only follow Ada's instructions if

This is my will, Babbage:

Get money from my mother, to be spent on the projects we have discussed.

Get my bank to give you the balance currently in my account.

Take charge of all my property and papers, and do whatever you like with them.

A. A. L.

Annabella agreed. And did she? Absolutely not.

In fact, Annabella was so furious that Ada had trusted Babbage over her own mother that Babbage was **never allowed to see Ada again**. Ada was distraught. Her last link with her dearest friend had been cut and there was nothing she could do about it.

Annabella didn't stop there. The weaker Ada became, the more her mother cut her off from anyone else who could support her. She even persuaded William that if Ada had any chance at all, it was only through her own nonstop care. **He needed permission to visit his own wife** in his own home.

Ada's daughter, young Annabella, was allowed to help look after her mother. Young Byron, now sixteen, was summoned from his ship (he'd been in the Royal Navy for three years). However, Ralph, now thirteen, was at school in Switzerland. While Ada could send him speedy messages by telegraph, getting the boy back to London, to her bedside, took a lot longer.

Only people on Annabella's approved list got to see Ada: certain family members, doctors, some of Annabella's friends . . . and the Furies.

Ralph finally arrived on August 26, and Ada seemed better for having all her children at her side. She'd had her ups and downs with them in the past, but they really mattered to her.

Ada clung to life for another three months. Three long months of Annabella's fussing, and no friends allowed, until, finally, she died on November 27, 1852.

Annabella must have grieved for her, but maybe she also breathed a small sigh of satisfaction. She had had Ada under her control right until the end!

Or had she . . . ?

POETRY AND SCIENCE TOGETHER

Ada gave William very precise instructions about how and where she wanted to be buried, and for once the law was in her favor. He was Ada's husband and he didn't have to ask for Annabella's permission. It turned out that, on their visit to Newstead two years earlier, **Ada had made a plan** and she'd got permission to be buried in the family vault of the local church.

Strangely, her father had been the same age as Ada when he died—just thirty-six—but thanks to the many developments in technology, the journey that Byron took to his final resting place was very different from the one that Ada took twenty-eight years later.

- 🖉 **Date:** July 1824
- 🖉 **Method of transport:** horse-drawn hearse all the way from London
- 🖉 **Time it took:** three days

ADA'S FUNERAL PROCESSION

- 🖉 **Date:** December 1852
- 🖉 **Method of transport:** Midland Railway Company most of the way; horse-drawn hearse from the station
- 🖉 **Time it took:** a few hours

While all Ada's friends were there, the Furies weren't—Ada had to die to get rid of them completely! Just two family members didn't make it. Young Byron was stuck back on his ship, and **Annabella "stayed away."** By being buried at her father's home, Ada had finally slipped out of Annabella's control. She'd always refused to take Ada to Newstead, so to show up now would have been a total humiliation.

Ada's coffin was covered in violet velvet and studded with silver coronets and the Lovelace arms. On the lid was the Lovelace motto that seemed to fit the way Ada had lived her life.

Augusta Ada King-Noel
Countess of Lovelace
December 10, 1815–November 27, 1852
Labor ipse voluptas

Finally, Ada was laid to rest next to her father. She'd never known him, yet in the end she had felt closer to the man who had given her an imagination than to her mother, who had tried so hard to suppress it.

There's no record of how Annabella felt, but it would be nice to think that at some point she realized she should be proud for bringing up a daughter who had **the mind of a scientist and the imagination**

of a poet. Ada was a daughter both parents should have been proud of. A daughter who would not be forgotten.

After Ada

Sadly, the Victorian computer age never happened. Difference Engine No. 2 and the Analytical Engine were never made—at least, not in Ada's or Babbage's lifetime. Babbage took up other causes, but he was tinkering with the design of the Analytical Engine until the day he died, in 1871, at age seventy-nine.

Over 100 years later, some engineers dug out the designs for Difference Engine No. 2 and there are now two fully working models of the machine, one in the Science Museum in London, and the other in Seattle. The machine works exactly as Babbage and Ada said it would.

The Analytical Engine never even got off the ground, unfortunately, but the idea didn't die.

And the *idea* of machines . . .

That can do things on their own.

That can think.

That can process information and create art and compose music . . .

All that came from Ada.

And There's More . . .

Ada lived in an age of clockwork and steam power. If only she'd made it to the ripe old age of eighty-nine, she might have witnessed the development that could make her ideas a reality:

1904—The invention of the vacuum tube finally made modern computers possible. It does the same thing in a computer as a wheel in the Analytical Engine, but much more quickly.

Wheel, used in Analytical Engine: makes things happen in a few seconds by turning.

Vacuum tube, used in early computers: makes things happen instantly by controlling electric current flow.

1930s and 40s—Modern computers really took off during and after World War II. Computer science was invented at this time, and technicians began to understand concepts like programming, processing, and memory.

Colossus Mark 2: one of the computers that helped the Allies win World War II.

Take that, Hitler!

1940s and 1950s—Vacuum tubes were replaced by transistors. Computers got smaller and faster. Computer scientists worked out that if you're processing numbers, you can process anything. Just as Ada had predicted.

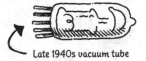

Late 1940s vacuum tube

Early 1950s transistor

1953—Ada's Notes were rediscovered and republished. All those modern computer scientists were shocked to discover that their ideas weren't new after all. Someone had got there 100 years before them—and that someone was a woman. Ada finally began to get the fame she deserved.

1960s—Silicon chips started to replace transistors. Computers got even smaller and even faster.

Unbelievable!

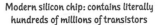

Mid-1950s transistor

Modern silicon chip: contains literally hundreds of millions of transistors

1970s—The American government started developing its own computer language for all its projects. They named it Ada in Countess Lovelace's honor, and even included her birth year in the specification number: MIL-STD-1815. Today Ada is the language used by air traffic control systems around the world, so you could say that Ada finally did get to fly!

They've developed flyology!

1980s—Commands started to be made using pictures (or graphical interfaces) rather than text.

Well, of course!

1990s–2000s—Next, came handheld digital devices . . .

Music, text, and pictures reduced to numbers in a machine's memory—just as I knew they could be.

1998—The British Computer Society released the Lovelace Medal, given to "individuals who have made an outstanding contribution to the understanding or advancement of Computing." The 2018 winner was Professor Gordon Plotkin, for his work on computer programming languages

2009—The first Ada Lovelace Day was celebrated, "to raise the profile of women in science, technology, engineering, and math." Ada was never taken quite as seriously as male mathematicians of her day. Now, Ada Lovelace Day is celebrated the second Tuesday of every October.

Yesss!

Ada's life was far too short, and while she lived, acknowledgement of her work and her genius was almost nonexistent. Perhaps if she'd been a man then people would have listened more carefully to her very original ideas.

Today, though, her name is known worldwide and her amazing achievements are rightfully recognized. Despite prejudice against her, and despite her physical and mental illness, she fought on through and planted the ideas that **made computer science possible**.

Ideas survive even if people die. Look around you: how much of what you can see depends on computers?

That's Ada's legacy. Over 160 years so far, and counting.

Timeline

So little time . . .
yet so much achieved!

1815
George Gordon Byron
(Lord Byron) and Anne
Isabella Milbanke marry.

December 10, 1815
Augusta Ada Byron (a.k.a. Ada
Lovelace) is born.

| 1815

| 1820

1816
Baby Ada is "stolen" by
Annabella, and Lord Byron
flees to Europe.

1824
Lord Byron dies.

1829
Ada gets the measles—and doesn't recover for three years!

| 1825

| 1830

1833
At age seventeen, Ada is presented to the king and officially becomes a young lady.

Ada meets Charles Babbage and is entranced by his Difference Engine.

1828
Ada develops "flyology."

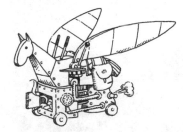

1835

Ada meets and marries
Lord William King.

Ada places her first bet.

1836

Ada's first son,
Byron, is born.

| 1830 | 1835 |

1837

Ada's daughter, Annabella,
is born.

Ada catches cholera.

1838

Ada becomes Lady
Augusta Ada King-Noel,
Countess of Lovelace.

1842

Luigi Federico Menabrea publishes an article about the Analytical Engine in French.

Ada translates the article and adds her own Notes at the end.

1839

Ada's second son, Ralph, is born.

| 1840

| 1845

1843

Ada writes to Charles Babbage offering to become his project manager for the Analytical Engine. He refuses.

Ada's translation of Menabrea's article with her Notes is published.

SKETCH
OF THE
ANALYTICAL ENGINE
INVENTED BY
CHARLES BABBAGE, Esq.
BY L. F. MENABREA,
of Turin,
OFFICER OF THE MILITARY ENGINEERS.
WITH NOTES BY THE TRANSLATOR.
[Extracted from the "SCIENTIFIC MEMOIRS," vol.III]

1848
Ada gets sick again.

1845
Ada works on her Calculus of the Nervous System.

| 1845

| 1850

1850
Ada and William visit Newstead Abbey, where Byron lived. Ada feels a connection with her father.

Come on, giddyap!

1851
Ada loses thousands of pounds betting on horses at the Derby.

Ada and William visit the Great Exhibition in London.

Ada develops cancer.

1852

Annabella bans Ada and Charles Babbage from seeing each other after Ada tries to give Babbage all her money and property.

November 27, 1852
Ada dies.

1855

1955

1953

Ada's Notes are rediscovered and republished, and finally she begins to get the recognition she deserves!

Glossary

agriculture: Farming, that includes growing crops and breeding animals for food, wool, and other products.

algebraic: Related to algebra (math where letters and other symbols represent numbers). $\frac{x}{e^x-1}=\sum_{n=0}^{\infty}\frac{B_n x^n}{n!}$

analytical: Involving detailed examination and investigation of something.

ancestor: a person from an earlier generation of the same family, or an earlier model of a machine.

antiseptic: Something that stops the spread of germs which cause disease.

aristocratic: Being part of a noble family in a high social position.

atom: The very smallest building block of every material that exists.

British Empire: A large group of countries that used to be ruled by the United Kingdom, including India, Canada, and Australia.

calculus: A branch of math that finds patterns between similar sums and uses formulas to help understanding.

chemistry: A type of science that studies the properties of different substances—what they're made up of, why they behave the way they do, and what happens when you combine them.

computer software: Programs and operating systems that tell a computer how to perform a task.

cube: To multiply a number by itself three times (for example, 2 x 2 x 2 = 8, which can be written as: $2^3 = 8$).

electric current : A flow of electric energy.

eligible: Allowed to participate in an activity.

engineering: Designing and making complicated products using math and science.

equation: A sum where both sides of the equals sign have the same value, e.g., $^1/_2 = ^2/_4$ or 1 + 5 = 3 + 3

formula: A mathematic or scientific rule or statement, written using letters and symbols.

hardware: The physical parts of a computer system.

hearse: A carriage that takes a coffin (and the body inside it) to a funeral or burial site.

intellect: The ability to reason and understand.

legacy: Money, property, a reputation, or ideas that are passed down as part of your history, or remaining from an earlier time.

$1674 \div \frac{14}{7} \times 389{,}217 \div 0.000042$

logical: Based on clear reasoning.

manufacturer: Someone who makes products, usually by machine, but sometimes by hand.

menagerie: A collection of animals, usually wild or exotic.

molecule: A tiny unit of a substance, made of a group of two or more atoms.

nervous system: The network of nerves in the human body, and most animals—made up of the brain, spinal cord, nerves, and sense organs like eyes and ears—which controls how the body works.

new-fangled: The newest style—often very different from what is normal or expected.

oscillating: Swinging steadily back and forth.

physics: A type of science that studies matter, forces and their effects with the aim of understanding how the universe behaves.

pulley: A simple machine using a grooved wheel and cord that makes lifting an object easier.

rank : Position in society.

shilling: A coin used in England from the 1500s to 1970—20 shillings made up one pound.

solitaire: A game for one person played with pegs on a board.

spouse: Husband or wife; partner in marriage.

statics: A branch of math that studies objects or bodies at rest.

status: Position in relation to other people in society.

suitor: A man who seeks a relationship with a particular woman with the aim of marrying her.

textiles: Cloths and fabrics.

tinkerer: Somebody who repairs and experiments (or tinkers) with machines.

vaccination: An injection that helps the body to prevent a particular infection.

vault: A chamber in a church or graveyard where bodies are buried.

vengeance: Punishing, or taking revenge on someone, for having wronged someone else.

visionary: Someone who uses imagination and wisdom to think about the future.

I never am really satisfied that I understand anything.

139

NOTES

7 "I awoke . . . famous": Thomas Moore, *Letters and Journals of Lord Byron*. London: J. Murray, 1830; page 159.

34 "Every moment . . . is born": Alfred, Lord Tennyson, "The Vision of Sin" in "Tennyson's poems: The Vision of Sin." *GradeSaver*. See www.gradesaver.com/tennysons-poems/e-text/the-vision-of-sin.

34 "I believe . . . poetry": Doron Swade, *The Difference Engine*. New York: Penguin Books, 2002; page 77.

42 "Whatever number . . . difference": Charles Babbage, *The Life of a Philosopher*. Cambridge: Cambridge University Press, 2011; page 65.

73 "It demonstrates . . . anticipate": Benjamin Woolley, *The Bride of Science*. New York: McGraw-Hill, 2000; page 267.

74 "The Analytical Engine . . . and leaves": Betty A. Toole, *Ada, the Enchantress of Numbers*. Moreton-in-Marsh, UK: Strawberry Press, 1998; page 182.

80 "I would . . . at you!": Toole, *Ada, the Enchantress of Numbers*, page 154.

81 "She is . . . exerted": Sydney Padua, *The Thrilling Adventures of Lovelace and Babbage*. New York: Pantheon, 2015; pages 274–275.

91 "Unfortunately . . . nothing more": Toole, *Ada, the Enchantress of Numbers*, page 230.

93 "I shall . . . brain": Toole, *Ada, the Enchantress of Numbers*, page 214.

101 "produce . . . somethings": Woolley, *The Bride of Science*, page 340.

117 "I'd rather . . . any spirit": Woolley, *The Bridge of Science*, page 344.

139 "I never . . . understand anything": "Quotations by Ada Lovelace." Strange Wondrous Quotes and Quotations. See strangewondrous.net/browse/author/l/lovelace+ada.

Select Bibliography

Babbage, Charles. *The Life of a Philospher*. Cambridge, UK: Cambridge University Press, 2011.

Moore, Thomas. *Letters and Journals of Lord Byron*. London: J. Murray, 1830.

Padua, Sydney. *The Thrilling Adventures of Lovelace and Babbage: The (Mostly) True Story of the First Computer*. New York: Pantheon, 2015.

Swade, Doron. *The Difference Engine: Charles Babbage and the Quest to Build the First Computer*. New York: Penguin Books, 2002.

Tennyson, Alfred, Lord. "The Vision of Sin." Quoted in "Tennyson's Poems: The Vision of Sin." *GradeSaver*. See www.gradesaver.com/tennysons-poems/e-text/the-vision-of-sin.

Toole, Betty A. *Ada, the Enchantress of Numbers: Prophet of the Computer Age*. Moreton-in-Marsh, UK: Strawberry Press, 1998.

Woolley, Benjamin. *The Bride of Science: Romance, Reason, and Byron's Daughter*. New York: McGraw-Hill, 2000.

INDEX

Use these pages for a quick reference!

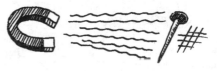

That's quite enough book learning for now.

Yes, be off with you!

About the Author

Ben Jeapes is a children's book author who also runs his own independent science fiction publishing house based in Abingdon, Oxfordshire.

About the Illustrator

Nick Ward is an illustrator, a writer, and the creator of several popular picture books for children. He lives in England.

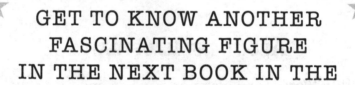

GET TO KNOW ANOTHER
FASCINATING FIGURE
IN THE NEXT BOOK IN THE

THE FIRST
NAMES SERIES

first names

MALALA
Yousafzai

NOBEL
PEACE PRIZE
2014

SCHOOL

NO GIRLS

"Don't tell me I can't go to school!"

Lisa Williamson ★ Illustrated by Mike Smith

Introduction

October 9, 2012
Mingora, Swat Valley, Pakistan

Malala was in a good mood traveling home from school. She was pretty sure she'd aced the test that morning and was looking forward to a relaxing afternoon at home.

She was laughing with her best friend, Moniba, when **the school bus stopped suddenly**. A young man was standing in the road. He wore long white robes and a baseball cap.

"Is this the Khushal School bus?" he asked.

Another young man jumped onto the back of the bus. A hush fell over the girls as both men glared at them. Heart hammering in her chest, Malala found Moniba's hand and gave it a squeeze. Around twenty girls were crammed onto the hard plastic benches and they stared back, stunned, as the men scanned the bus.

"Who is Malala?" the second man asked gruffly. No one answered, but a few of the girls glanced in Malala's direction before they could stop themselves. Then the same man **raised a pistol**.

Malala froze with fear.

The man fixed his gaze on her and aimed his pistol at her head. The other girls began to scream, but Malala didn't make a sound. She just squeezed Moniba's hand harder.

A split second later, the man pulled the trigger and **everything went black**.

Malala was bleeding profusely as the bus swerved through the heaving streets of Mingora, speeding toward the local hospital. Once there, doctors said her prospects were grim, so grim that with a heavy heart, Malala's dad **began making funeral arrangements**. For a short while it looked like the men had succeeded in their quest to silence her.

But Malala did not die; she survived, and within days of her shooting she had become one of most famous teenagers on the planet. And she was more determined than ever to stand up for what she believed in: that every single girl in the world deserved to go to school. And she wanted as many people to hear her message as possible. She has since written books, appeared on television, and met all sorts of important people, including President Obama and the Queen of England. She's also the youngest person ever to win the Nobel Peace Prize.

Incredible stuff, right?

> Yes, but I'm actually quite ordinary, you know.

Yeah, right! Didn't Beyoncé wish you a happy birthday once?

> Well, yes . . .

And Selena Gomez called you her "role model!"

> OK, OK, but I promise you the real Malala isn't all that different from other girls.

Really?

> Yes! I love television, and I argue with my brothers over stupid things, like the TV remote and who ate the last slice of pizza!

You like pizza?

> Oh yes! And curry. And cupcakes. Mmmmm, especially cupcakes . . . And I like reading and listening to music and shopping and hanging out with my friends. Oh, and I hate getting up in the morning!

Hmm, all of that does sound pretty ordinary, actually.

So what makes Malala's story so special? Well, it didn't start with the shooting and the sudden fame. This ordinary girl was destined to achieve **extraordinary things** from the very moment she was born.

1 No Party for Malala

Ziauddin Yousafzai was over the moon. On the hot sticky morning of July 12, 1997 his wife gave birth to their first child—a beautiful bouncing baby girl. Over the next few days, he was so excited that he told everyone he met about the new addition to his family. People were polite but confused.

Why was he so happy and proud? After all, his wife had **a baby girl**. The thing is, in Pakistan, even today, from the second they enter the world, boys and girls are mostly treated very differently. When a baby boy is born, the family celebrates. Guns are fired up into the sky and visitors come to coo over the cradle and cram it with sweets and money. But when a baby girl is born . . . no gunshots, no gifts—people don't even bother to visit! Instead they sympathize with the "poor" mother and hope, for her sake, that her next child will be a boy.

Girls play as important a role in Pakistan as they do anywhere else in the world, but some families see raising girls as **a financial burden**. Girls aren't allowed to go out to work and provide for their families like boys do, and it can cost over a million rupees (about $15,000) to marry a daughter off.

Most girls spend their lives at home being wives and mothers, cooking and looking after the house and their children. And for some reason, that doesn't seem as important as earning a regular income. This is the way it's been for hundreds of years, which is why Ziauddin's celebrating his daughter was so unusual.

That's my dad for you! With a different set of parents, I'd probably be married with at least two babies by now.

To get to know me, you need to understand them first . . .

HIGH-FLYING ZIAUDDIN

Ziauddin had a habit of challenging tradition that started when he was a boy—**and brother to five sisters!** While he and his older brother went off to school, the girls stayed at home and learned how to run a house, so that when they got married and had families of their own, they'd know what to do. Ziauddin thought this seemed **really unfair**, and as soon as he was old enough, he planned to do something about it.

But my dad had a really bad stutter, which made speaking in public unbelievably scary.

In spite of his stutter, Ziauddin entered a public speaking competition. He practiced and practiced and practiced until he knew his speech so well he could recite it in his sleep.

When the day of the competition rolled around, Ziauddin was terrified.

A-hem . . .

Read on in the next title in the
FIRST NAMES series:

MALALA YOUSAFZAI